EDGAR BRANDT. Detail from a five-paneled folding screen (Plate 4).

ART DECO
DECORATIVE IRONWORK

Henri Clouzot

DOVER PUBLICATIONS, INC.
Mineola, New York

Bibliographical Note

Art Deco Decorative Ironwork, first published by Dover Publications, Inc., in 1997, is a reprint of all 104 plates from *La Ferronnerie Moderne*, Editions d'Art Charles Moreau, Paris, 3 portfolios, n.d. The plates have been renumbered in order to keep each designer's work all together. The introductory note, captions and index were prepared specially for the Dover edition.

Library of Congress Cataloging-in-Publication Data

Clouzot, Henri, 1865–1941.
    Art deco decorative ironwork / Henri Clouzot.
        p.   cm.
    "The plates are reproduced in their entirety from La ferronnerie moderne, Editions d'Art Charles Moreau, Paris, 3 portfolios, n.d.; they have been repositioned for ease of reference, so that each designer's work is grouped together"—T.p. verso.
    Includes bibliographical references and index.
    ISBN 0-486-29812-4
    1. Ironwork—Europe—History—20th century—Pictorial works. 2. Decoration and ornament—Art deco—Pictorial works. 3. Subes, Raymond, 1893– Ferronerie moderne—Illustrations. I. Title.
NK8242.C57   1997
739.4'094'09042—dc21   95-16160
                                                        CIP

Manufactured in the United States of America
Dover Publications, Inc., 31 East 2nd Street, Mineola, N.Y. 11501

NOTE

The term Art Deco has its source in the "Exposition Internationale des Arts Décoratifs et Industriels Modernes" (Paris, 1925), an exhibition which offered its visitors the first comprehensive look at what was becoming a dominant style in the decorative arts. The Exposition brought together furniture, glassware, ironwork, textiles, and other products by many of the leading craftsmen of the day. These products were displayed in architect-designed pavilions such as the Pavillon du Collectionneur and the Pavillon de l'Elégance. Their work thus juxtaposed, it became readily apparent that many of the artists shared common sources as well as the beginnings of a common language of design: elements of Art Nouveau, Cubism, Expressionism, the Arts and Crafts and the Secessionist styles and even of ancient Egyptian and Aztec motifs could be seen reflected in their works. Highly stylized images such as rainbows, fountains, and sun rays recurred throughout their designs. With their frequently symmetrical, rectilinear forms and repeated geometric patterns, many of the objects also showed a particular suitability for mass production, thereby uniting the artistic with the industrial world.

The influence of Art Deco spread quickly in the years following the Exposition. Improvements in international transportation made it easier than ever before for foreign designers to visit the center of artistic activity in Europe, where they could see the artists' products in their studios and galleries, or study the architects' buildings in person. Books such as *La Ferronnerie Moderne* (from which the plates in this book are taken) and *L'Art International d'Aujourd'hui* helped broadcast the latest trends to the world, allowing artists in America, for instance, to see and to copy what their compatriots in Europe were doing, without ever having to leave home. Soon the designers of film sets, advertisements, and books began to imitate the Art Deco style, and from that point on its widespread dissemination and popularity were assured.

No other artistic style caught so well the spirit of those times, and perhaps no medium expressed so well the spirit of Art Deco itself as that of ironwork. A piece such as Edgar Brandt's folding screen "The Oasis" (frontispiece and plate 4), with its fountain jets, rainbows, and fronds reflected from one panel to the next, displays the symmetry of form as well as the stylized imagery that would come to exemplify Art Deco. It is a work of great beauty and craftsmanship, its iron hand-wrought (that is, shaped by hand on an anvil rather than cast in a mold) and then highlighted with gold, demonstrating with éclat that a functional, everyday piece of furniture could be at once practical, skillfully made, and attractive.

Brandt of course was not the only craftsman of his time to employ this medium: the pages that follow show off the talents of a multitude of designers who recognized the possibilities afforded by working in iron. The malleability of that metal makes it one of the most adaptable materials an artist can use. It can, as "The Oasis" shows, be shaped into a unique and individual form, with no two pieces exactly the same. It can also be cast again and again in a mold, one pattern repeated as often as a project requires. Iron can be coupled with glass, alabaster, marble, and wood (among other materials), increasing its possible uses manifold. With its strength, iron can be used indoors and out to make gateways, door grilles, lampposts, and railings; it can also be subtly worked into mirror frames, chandeliers, latches, and locks. Long a component of architectural and decorative design, iron constantly challenges the artist to invent new forms, to use the material in original and innovative ways. The examples that Henri Clouzot has gathered here provide ample evidence of the Art Deco designer's success in meeting that challenge.

TABLE OF CONTENTS

The bracketed roman numerals indicate the portfolio of *La Ferronnerie Moderne* in which each plate originally appeared.

1

2

1.   EDGAR BRANDT. Gateway (1, detail, and 2, full view).

1

2

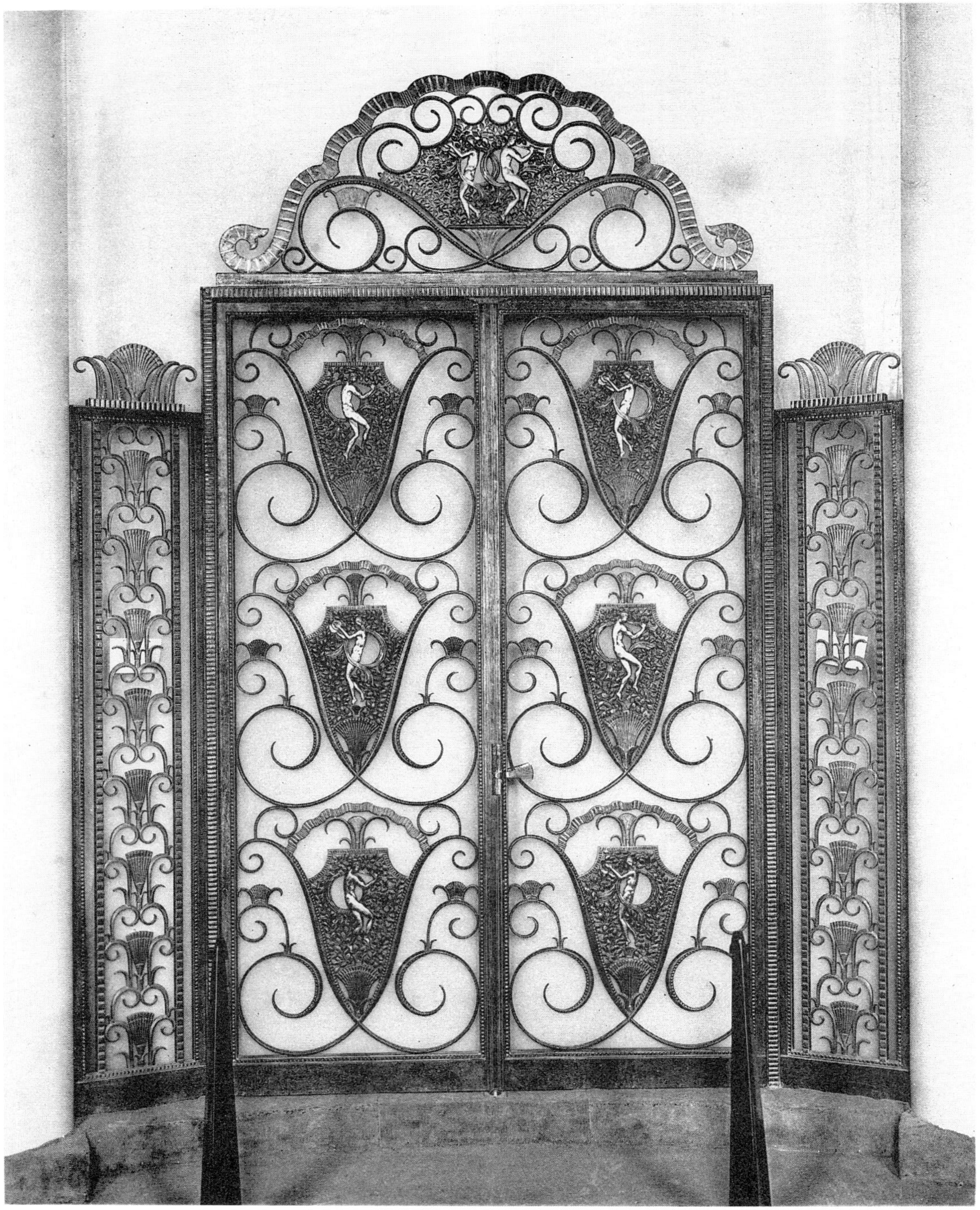

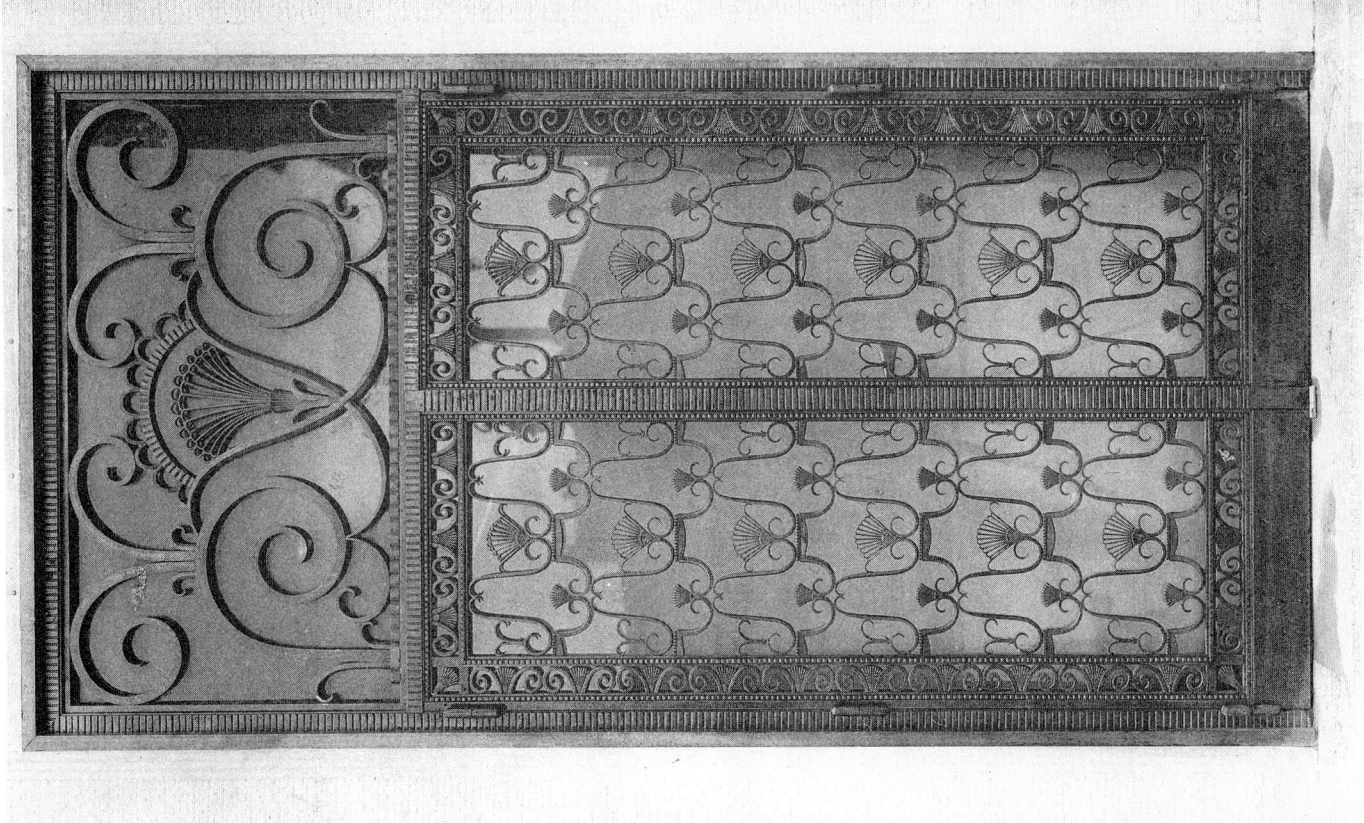

2. Edgar Brandt. (1) Interior grillwork and (2) entrance for the Pavillon du Collectionneur.

2

1

3.   EDGAR BRANDT. (1, 2) Interior grillwork, Pavillon du Collectionneur.

4.   EDGAR BRANDT. (1) Interior grillwork and torchères. (2) Five-paneled folding screen, "The Oasis," of wrought iron highlighted with gold.

1

2

3

5.   EDGAR BRANDT. (1, 2) Fireplace screens. (3) Console, Pavillon du Collectionneur.

1

2

3

6.   EDGAR BRANDT. (1, 2) Chandeliers. (3) Railing, Cour des Métiers.

2

1

7.   EDGAR BRANDT. (1) Doors, Pavillon national Monégasque. (2) Entrance, Pavillon du Collectionneur.

8.   Edgar Brandt. (1) Doors, Boutique de l'Illustration. (2) Entrance, Pavillon de la Renaissance.

1

2

9.   EDGAR BRANDT. (1, 2) Interior grillwork.

3

1

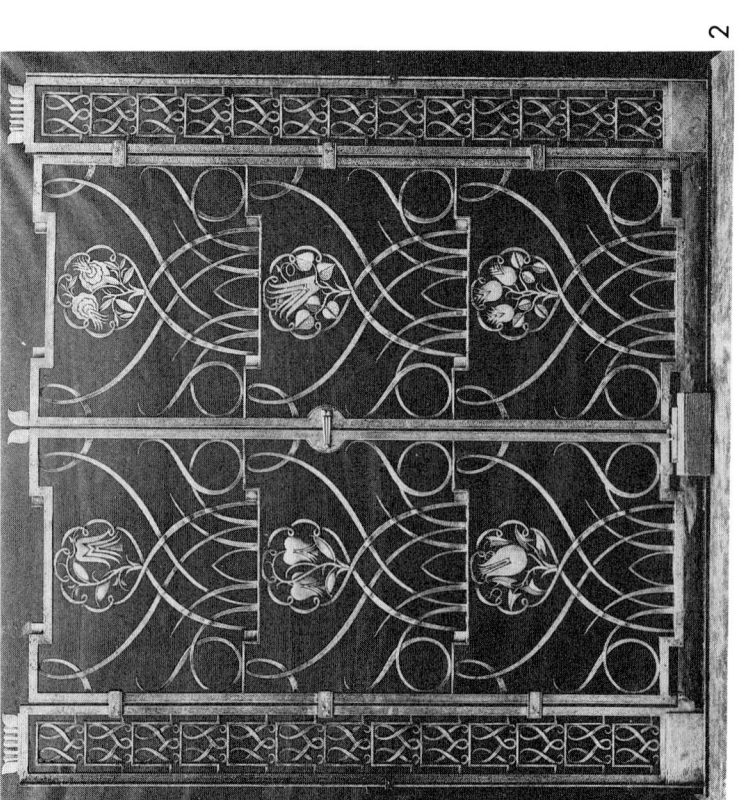

2

10. EDGAR BRANDT. (1) Fireplace screen. (2) Interior grillwork. (3) Bronze and wrought iron doors, Montreal Stock Exchange.

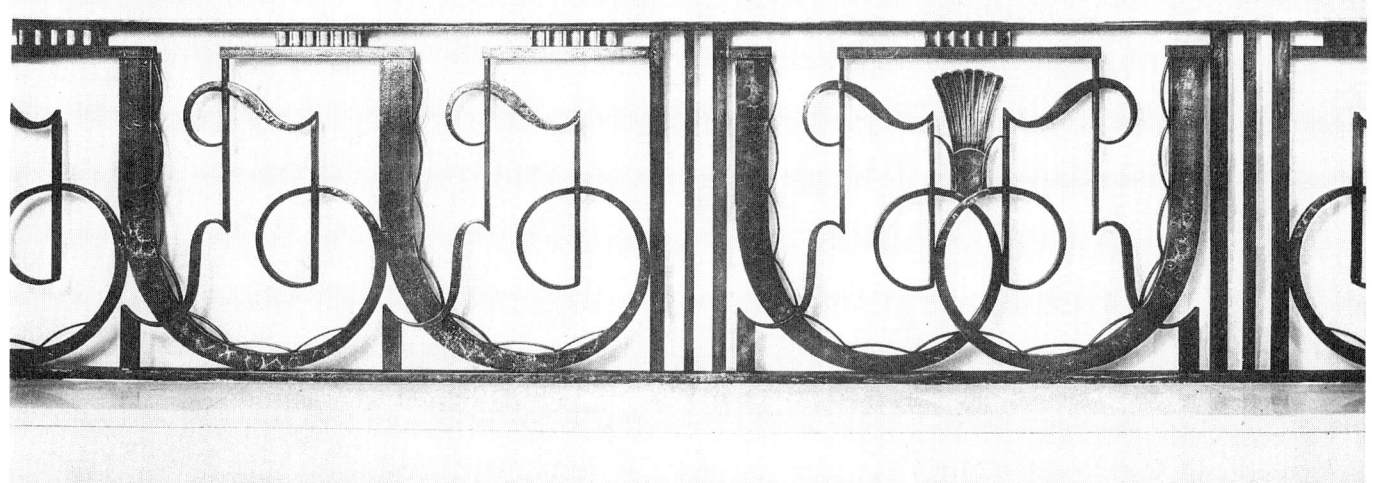

1

2

11.   EDGAR BRANDT. (1, 2) Wrought iron railings.

2

1

12.   EDGAR BRANDT. (1) Wrought iron banister. (2) Elevator doors.

13.   EDGAR BRANDT. (1, 2) Chandeliers.

1

2

3

14.   BAGUÈS FRÈRES. (1) Balcony, Pavillon de la Ville de Paris. (2) Railing and (3) balcony, Pavillon de l'Elégance.

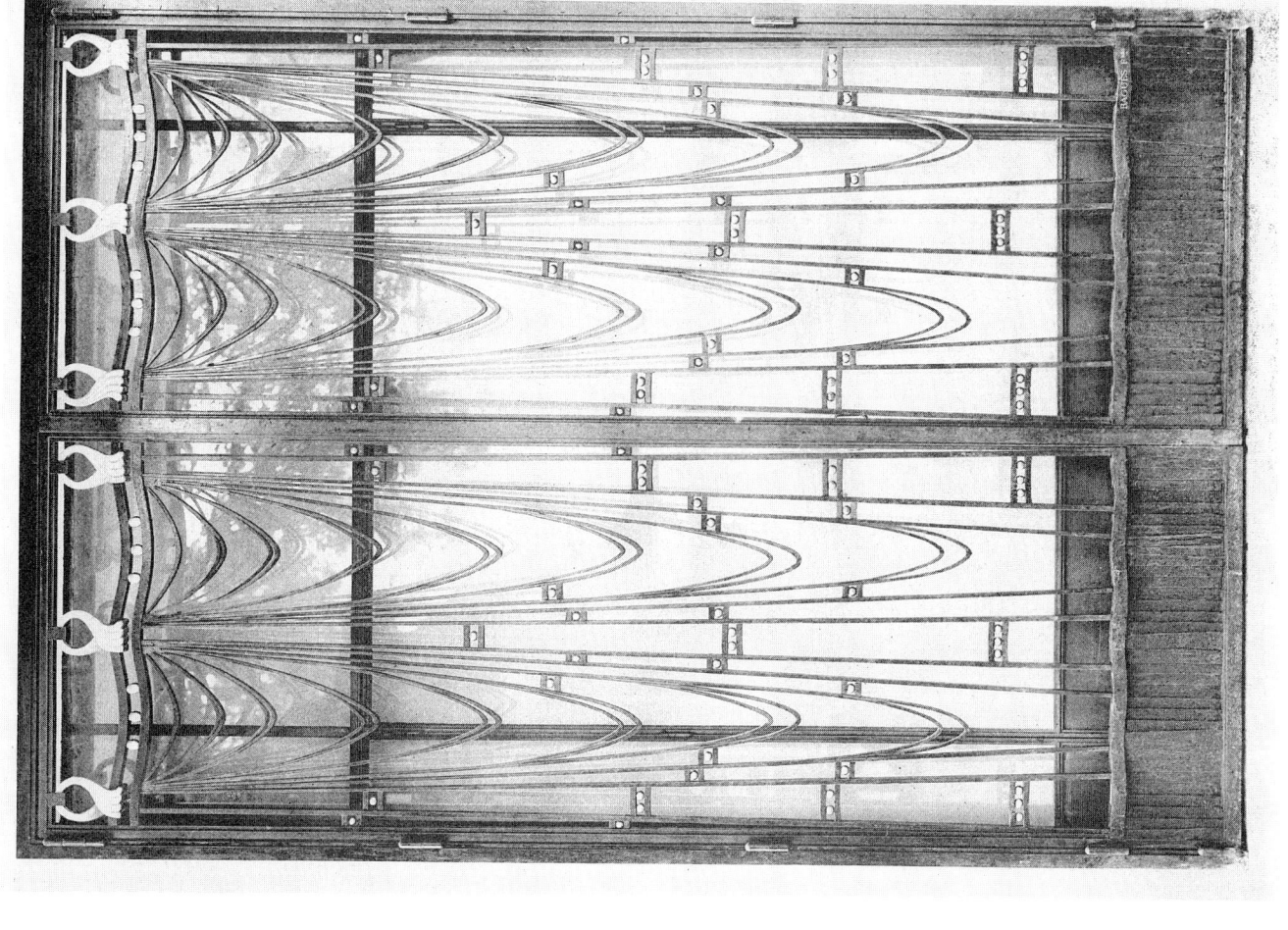

15.   BAGUÈS FRÈRES. (1) Entrance and (2) exit, Pavillon de l'Elégance.

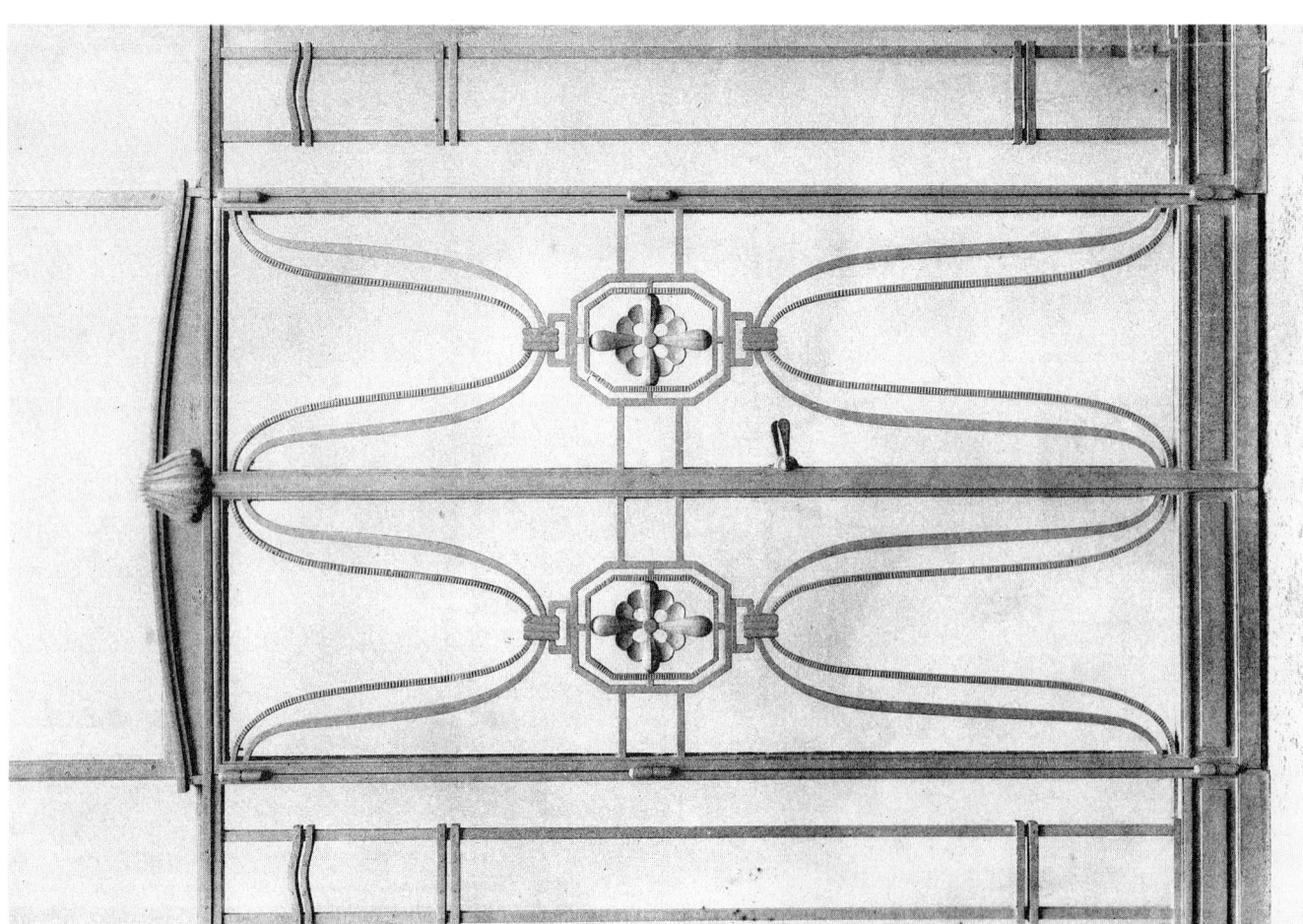

16.   BAGUÈS FRÈRES. (1) Interior door, Pavillon de la Ville de Paris. PAUL KISS. (2) Entrance, Pavillon Savary.

1

2

1

2

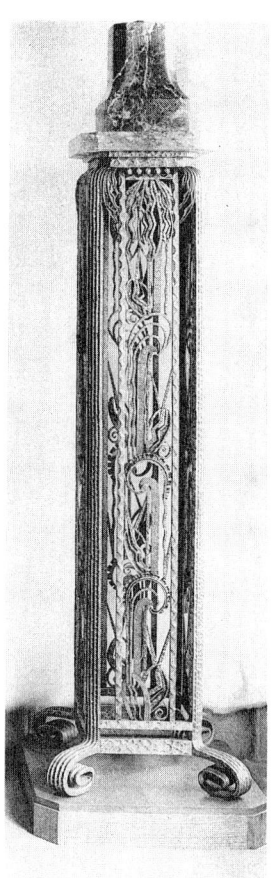

3

4

17.   PAUL KISS. (1, 3) Pedestals, (2) side table, and (4) interior grillwork, Pont Alexandre III boutique.

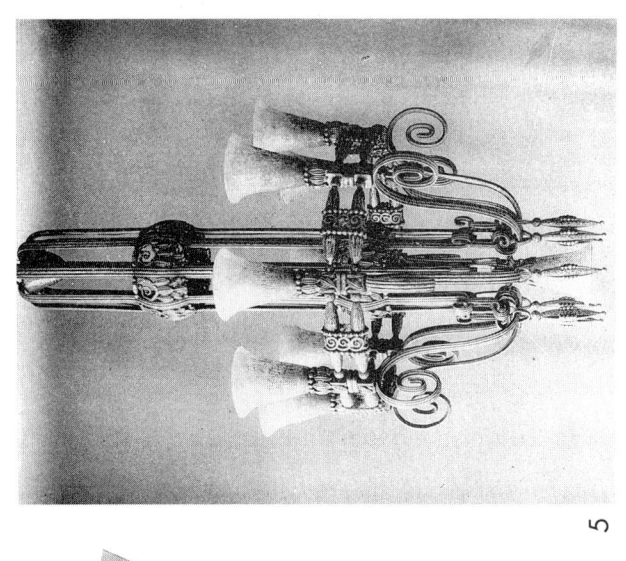

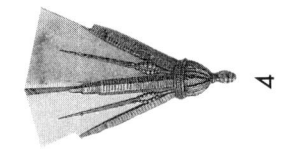

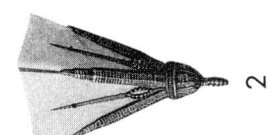

18. PAUL KISS. (1) Door, Monument aux Morts de Levallois-Perret. (2, 4) Wall sconces. (3) Console and mirror. (5) Chandelier. (6) Radiator cover.

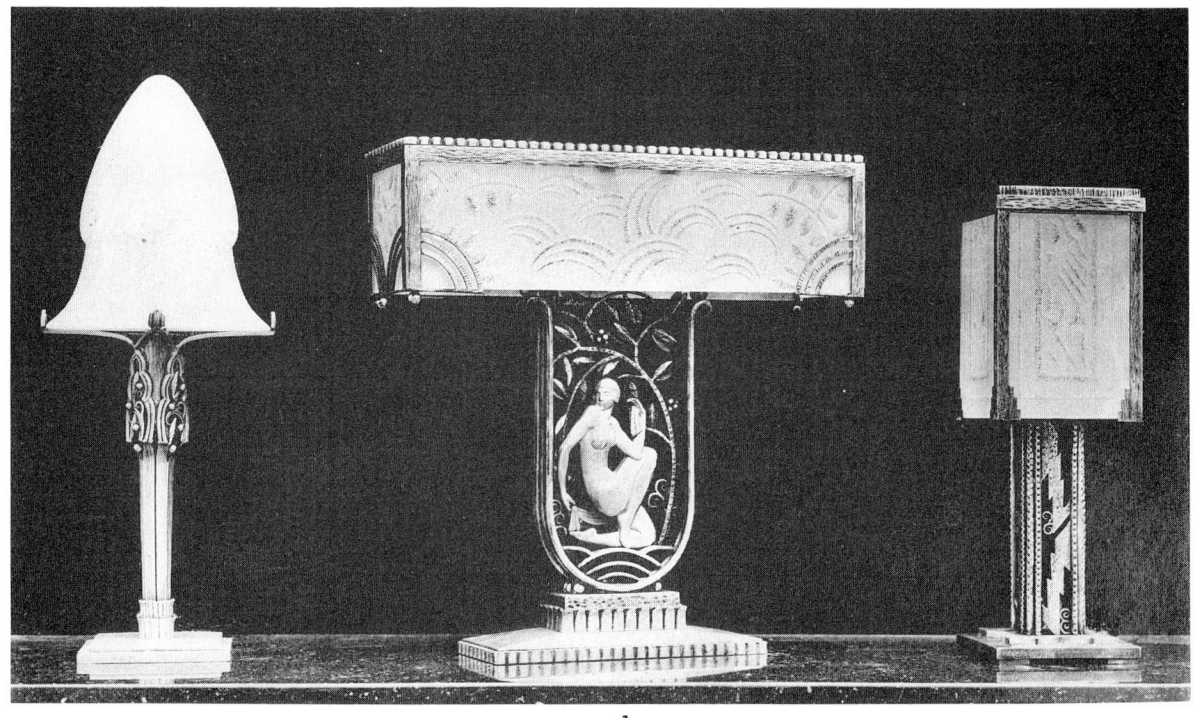

1

2

3

19.   PAUL KISS. (1) Table lamps. (2) Interior grillwork. (3) Floor lamp.

1

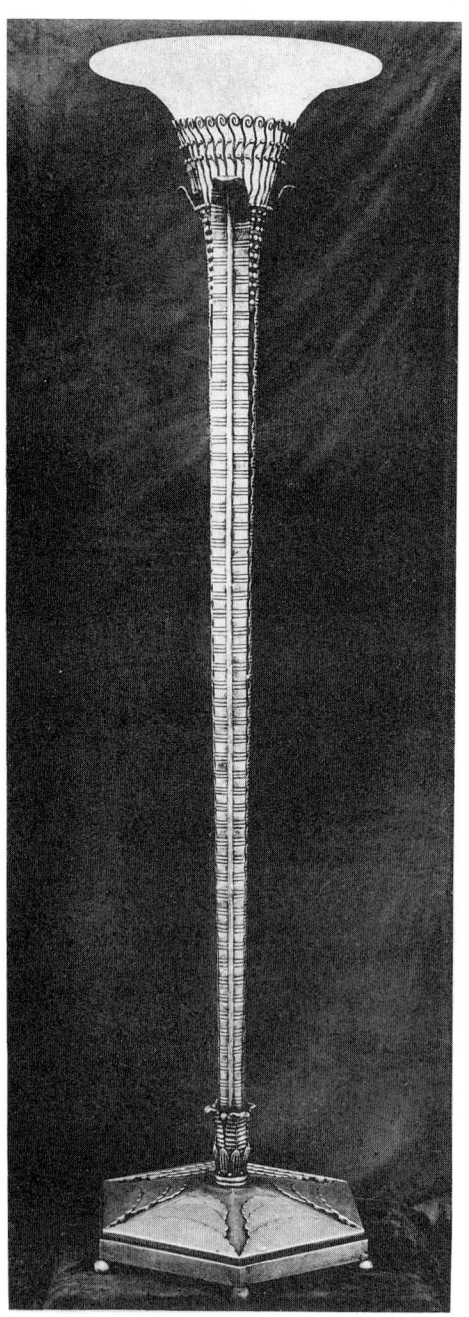

2

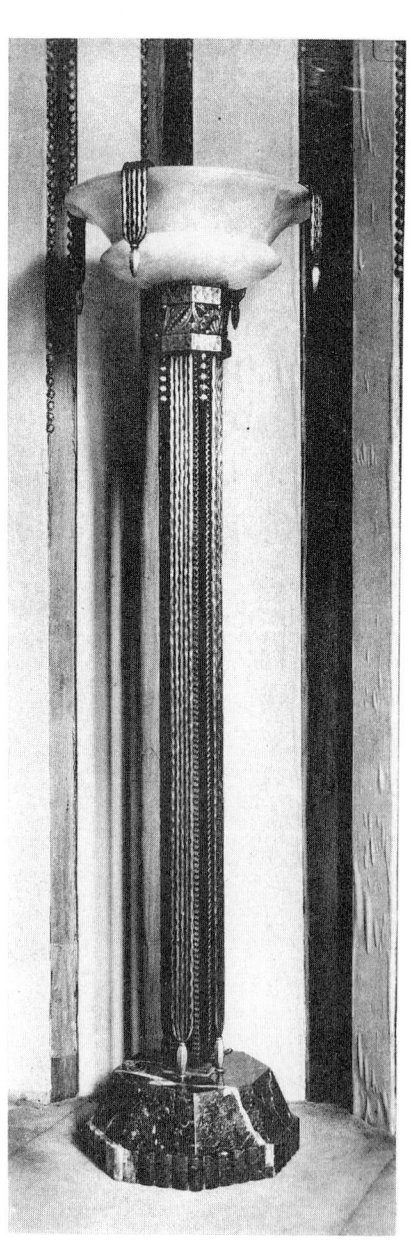

3

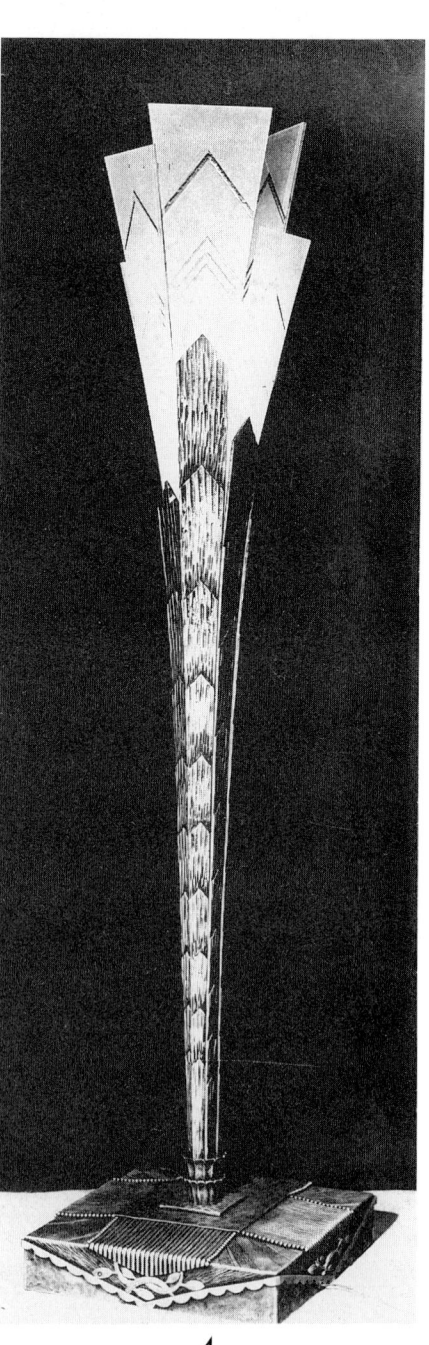

4

20.   PAUL KISS. (1) Interior grillwork. (2, 3) Torchères. (4) Floor lamp.

21.   PAUL KISS. (1) Desk. (2) Console and mirror. (3) Radiator cover.

1

2

3

22. PAUL KISS. (1) Interior grillwork. (2) Balustrade. (3) Five-paneled folding screen.

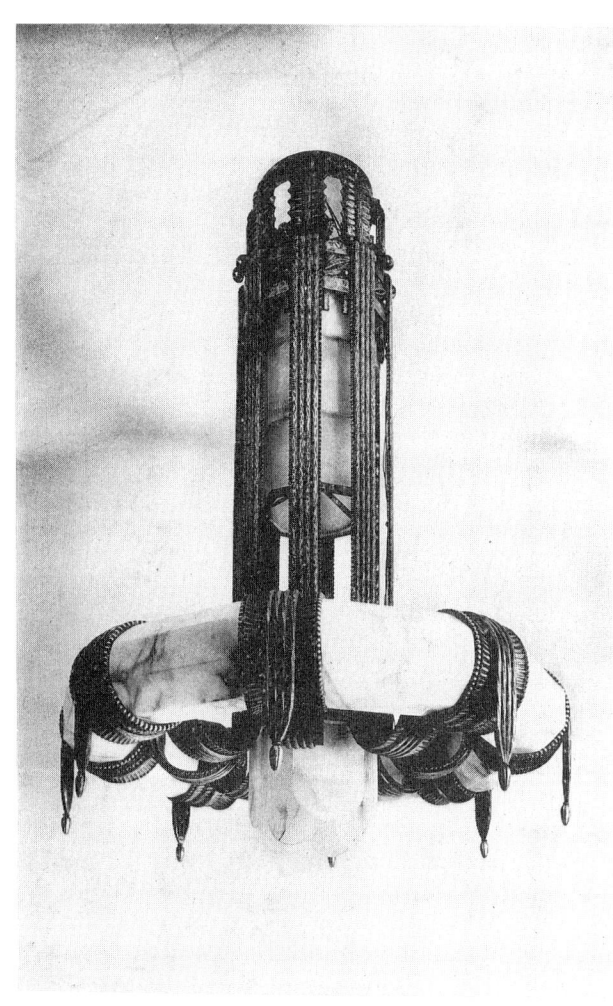

1

2

3

23.   PAUL KISS. (1) Chandelier. (2) Door. (3) Table lamps.

24.   VASSEUR. Dining room, Pavillon de la "Maitrise" (two views).

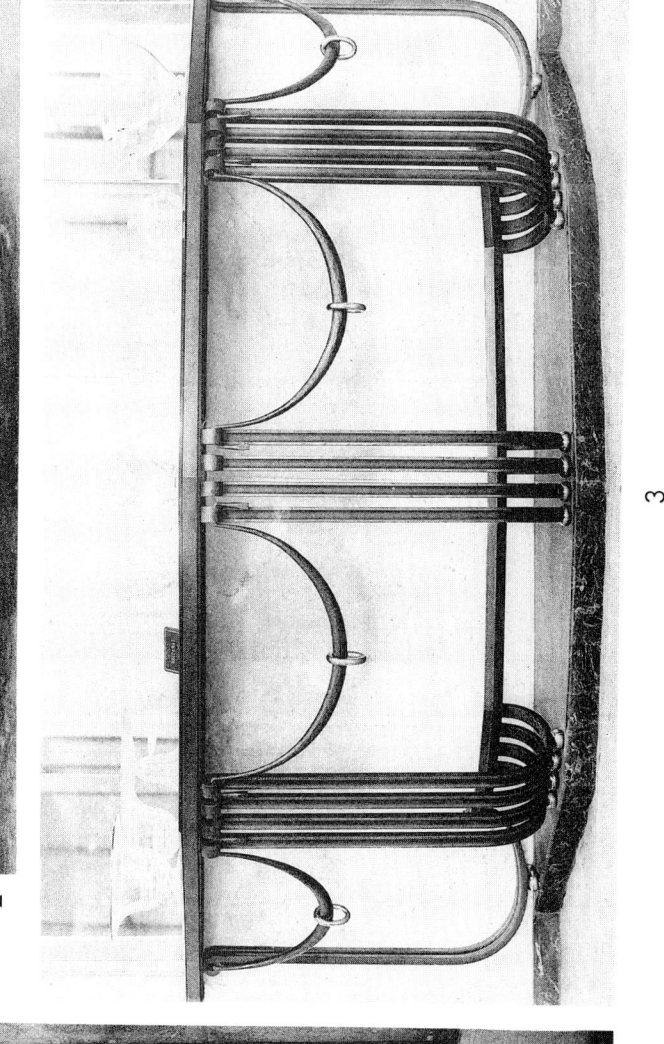

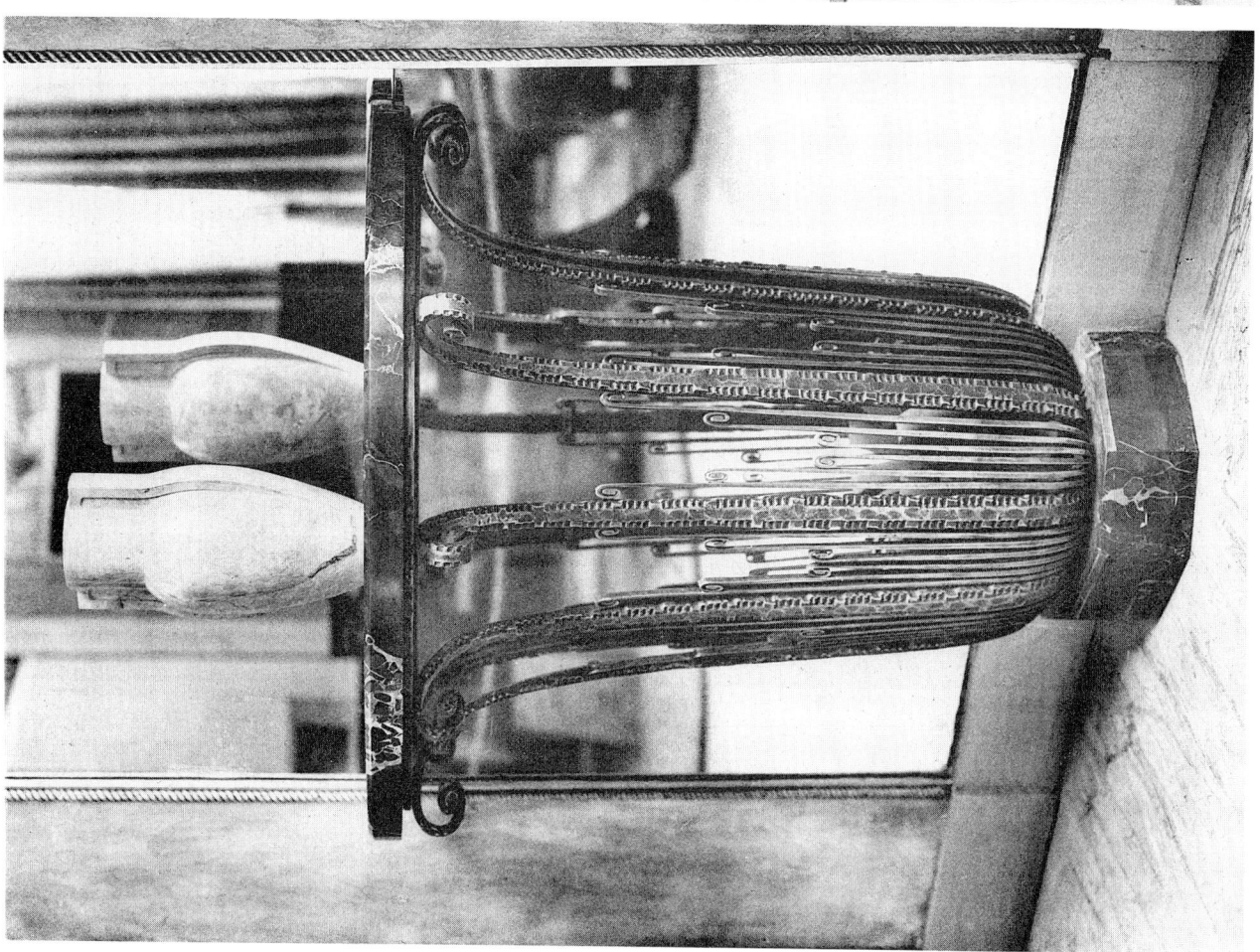

2

3

1

25.   RAYMOND SUBES (1), VASSEUR (2), CHRISTOFLE ET CIE. (3). Consoles.

2

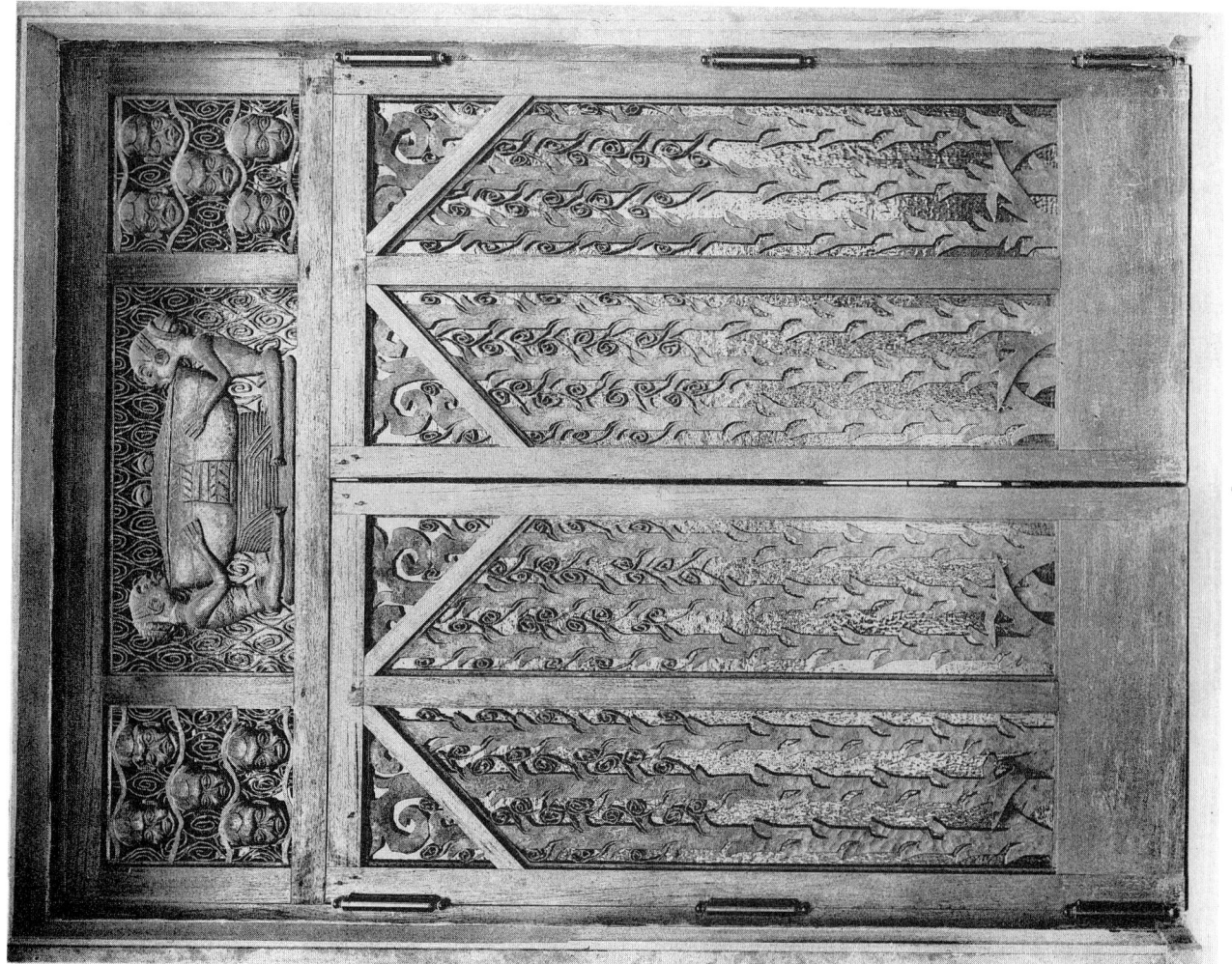

1

26. RAYMOND SUBES. Entrances, Pavillon de l'Afrique Française (1) and Pavillon du Club des Architectes diplomés (2).

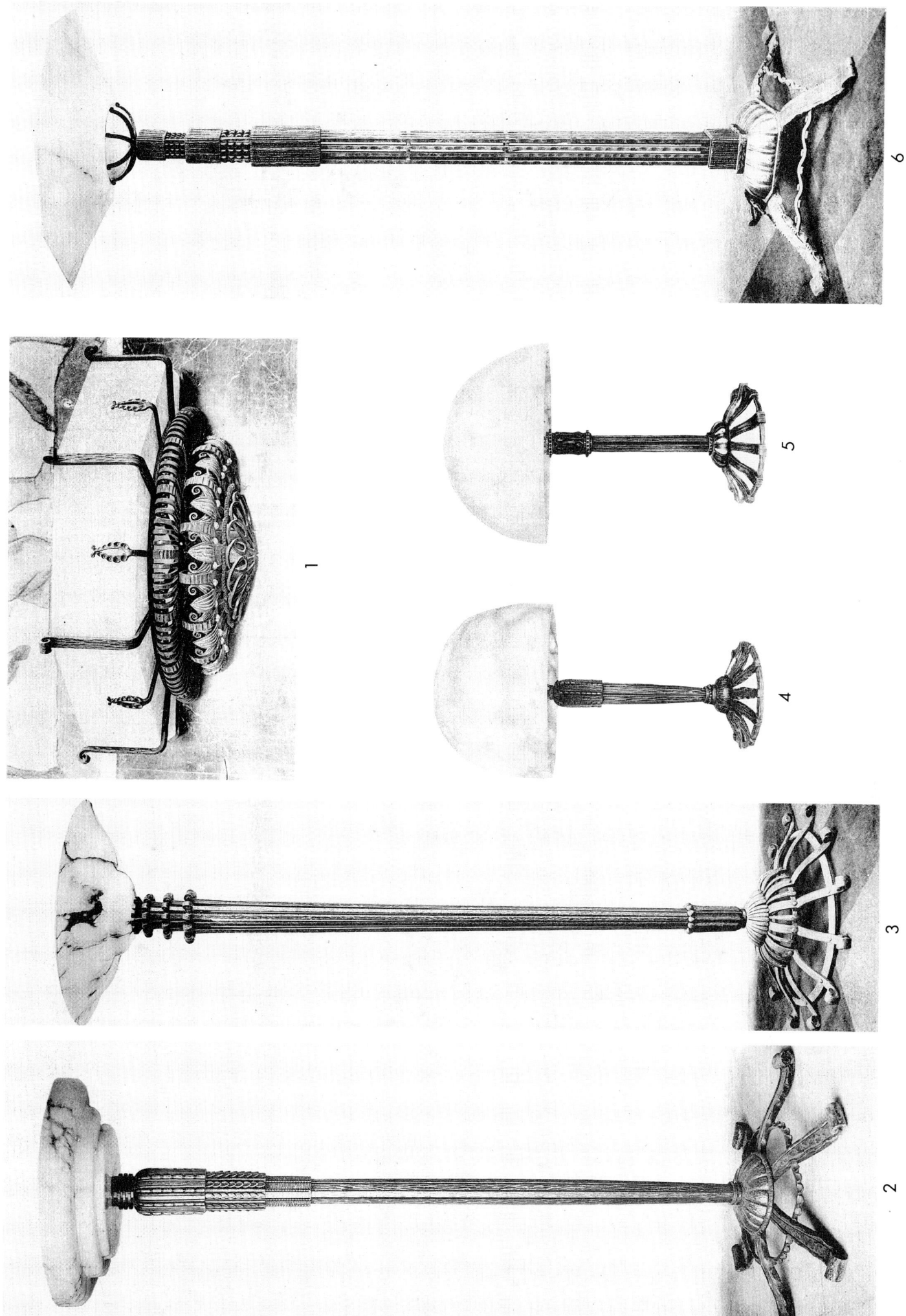

27. RAYMOND SUBES. (1) Wall sconce. (2, 3, 6) Floor lamps. (4, 5) Table lamps.

28.   RAYMOND SUBES. (1) Balcony. (2) Communion grille. (3, 4) Radiator covers.

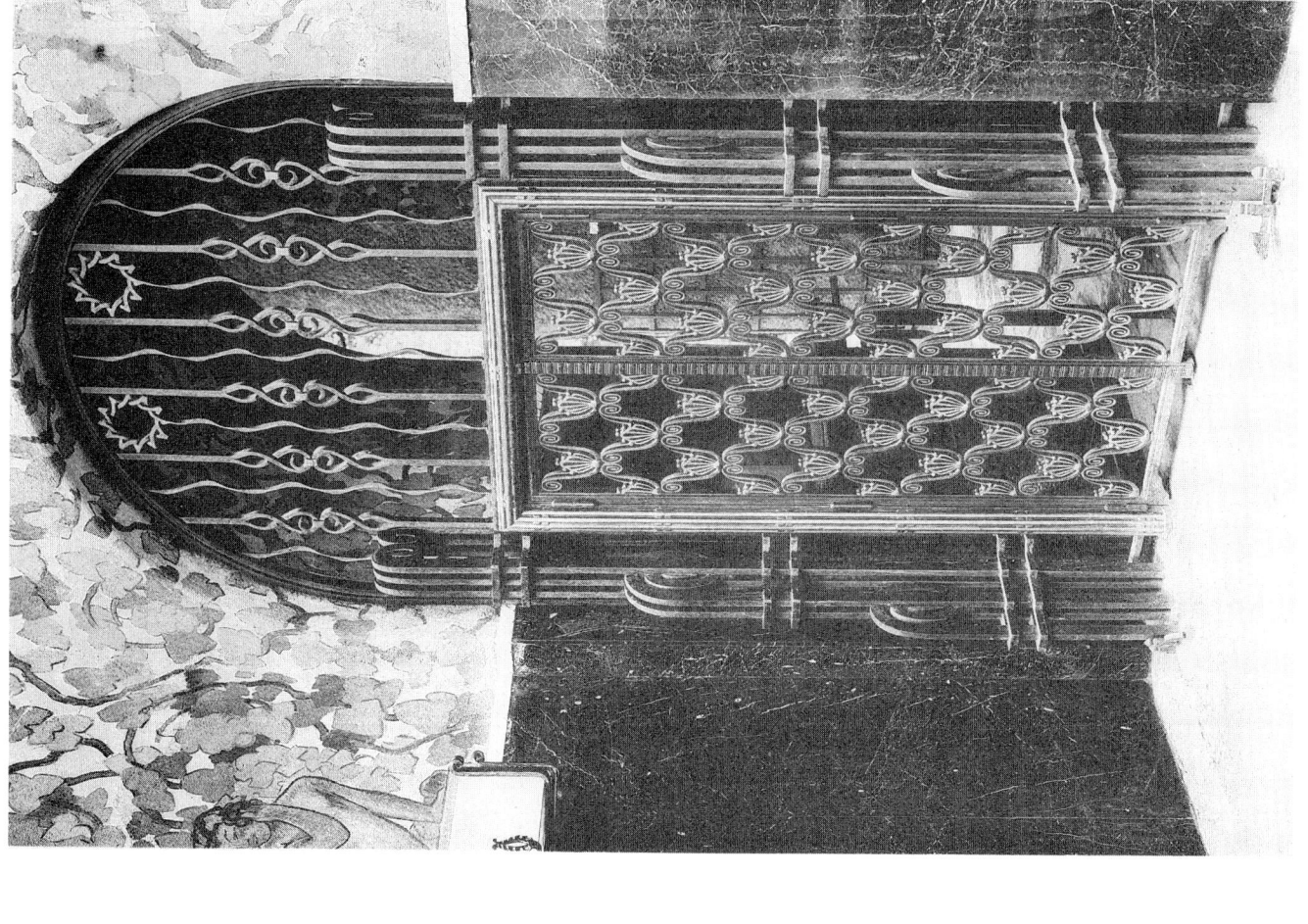

29. RAYMOND SUBES. (1, 2) Gates.

1

2

1

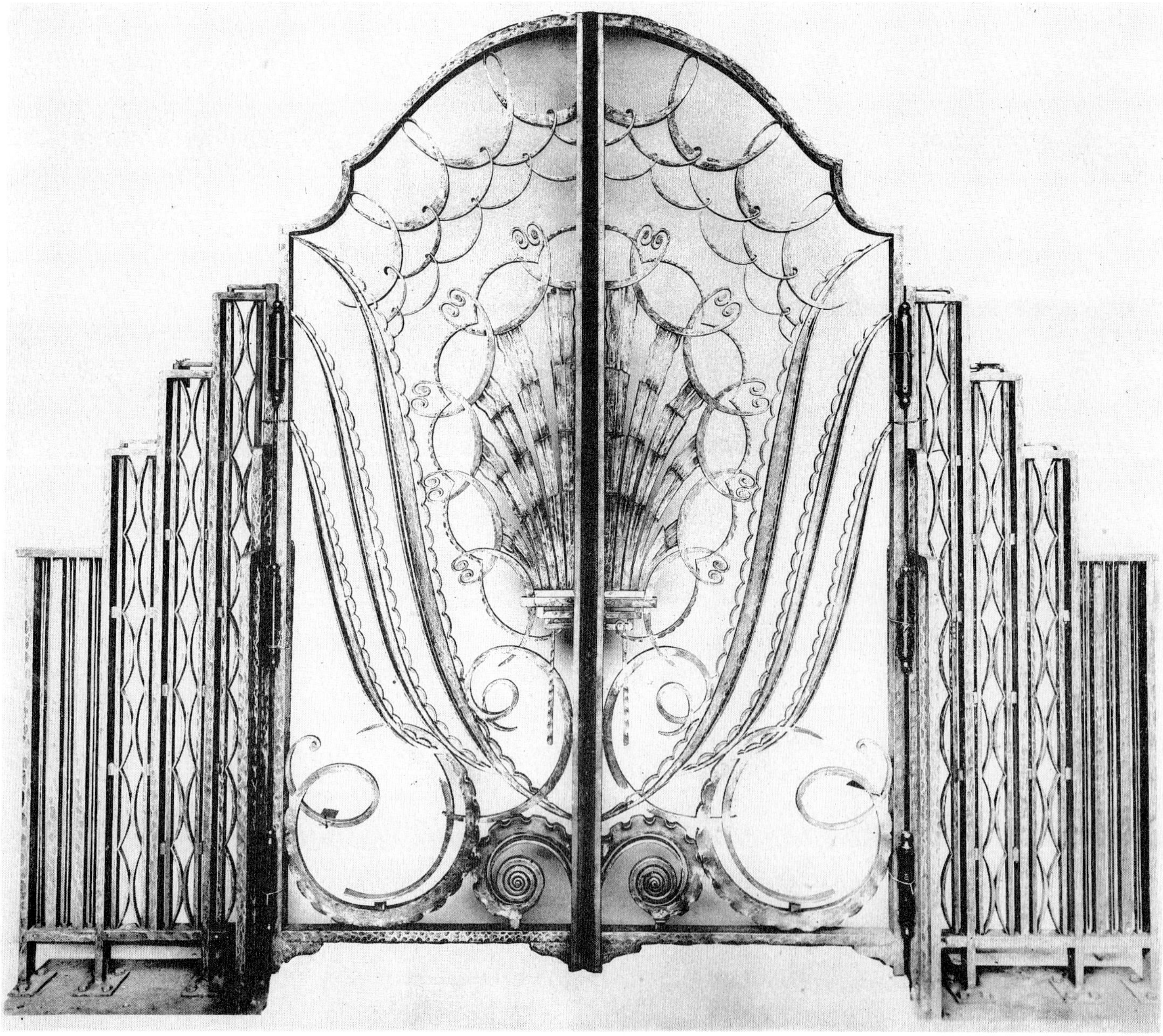

2

30.   RAYMOND SUBES. (1) Railing and (2) door for the luxury liner "Ile de France."

1

2

3

31. RAYMOND SUBES. (1, 2) Wrought iron wall sconces. (3) Console, mirror, and table lamps.

1

2

32.   RAYMOND SUBES. (1) Torchères, mirror, and railing. (2) Detail of railing.

1   2

3   4

33.   RAYMOND SUBES. (1) Vase with wrought iron framework. (2) Table lamp. (3, 4) Wall sconces.

1

2

34.   RAYMOND SUBES. (1) Banister. (2) Elevator door.

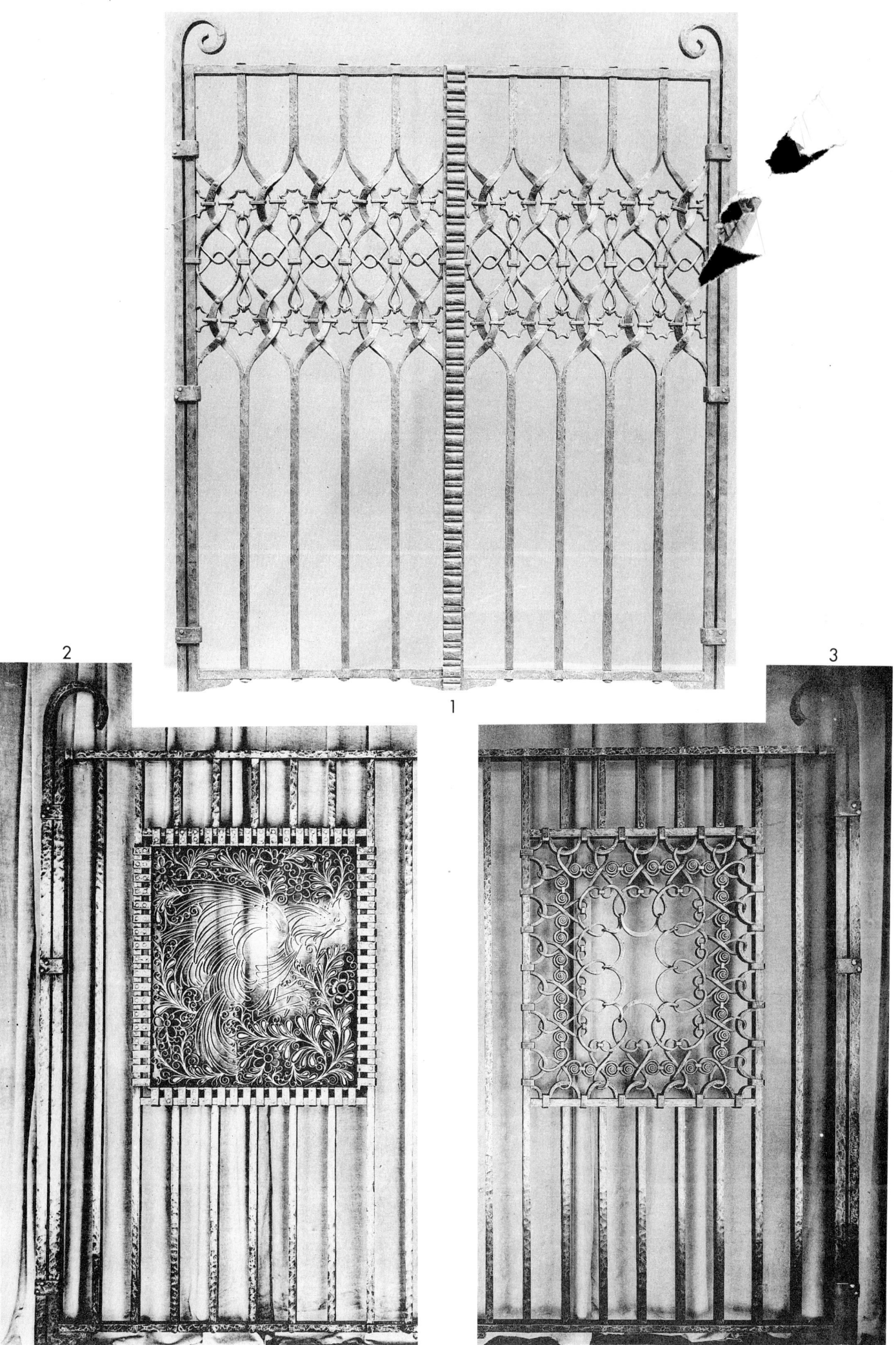

35.   RAYMOND SUBES. (1–3) Grillwork from park fences.

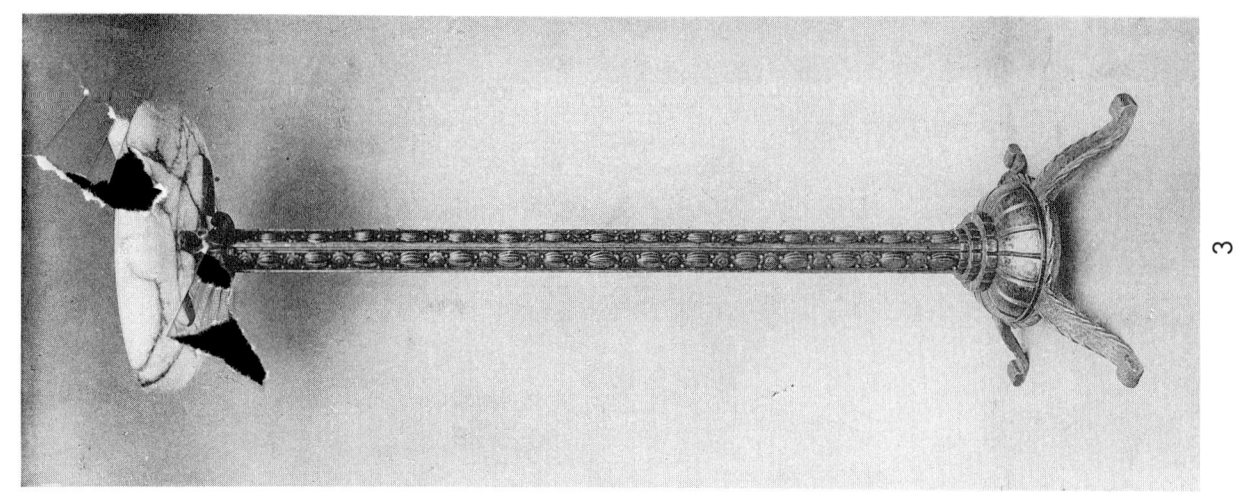

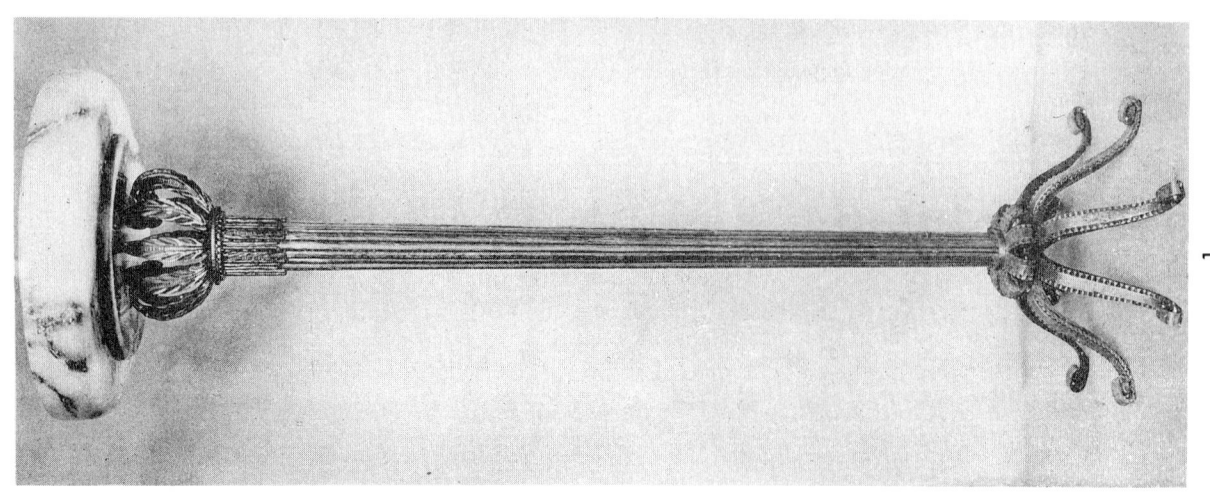

36.   RAYMOND SUBES. (1, 3) Torchères. (2) Console and framed mirror.

37. RAYMOND SUBES. (1) Chapel doors for the luxury liner "Ile de France." (2) Grillwork for an apartment block.

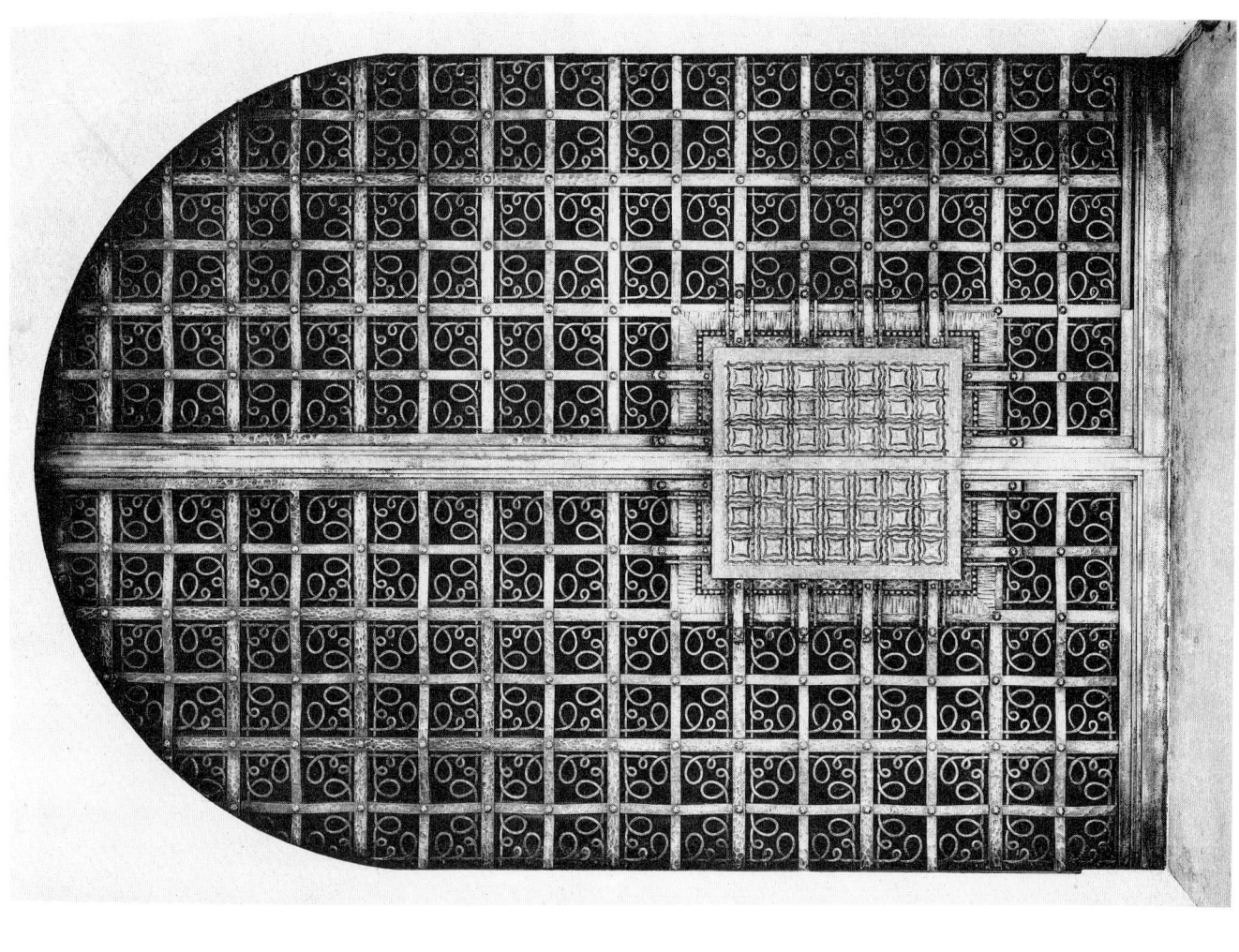

2

1

38.   RAYMOND SUBES. (1) Interior grillwork. (2) Grillwork for a bank.

1

2

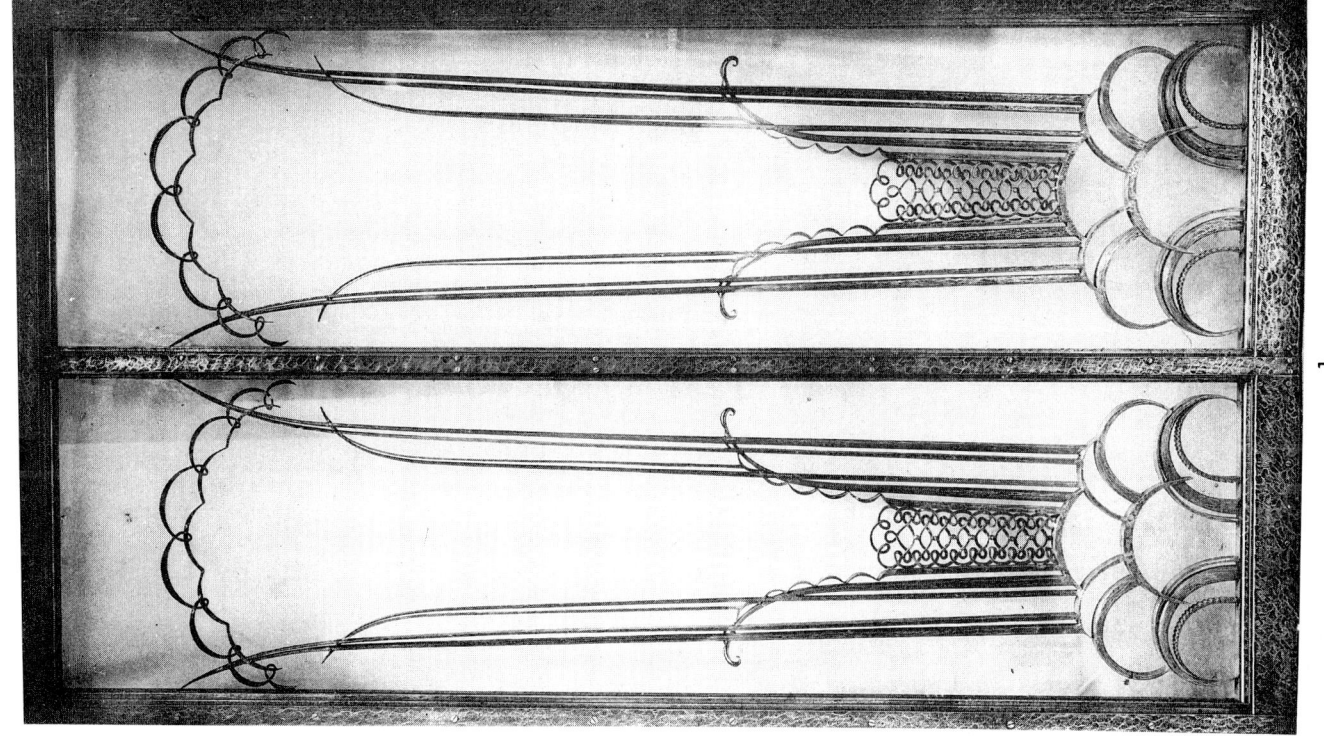

39. Raymond Subes. (1) Grillwork. (2) Building entrance.

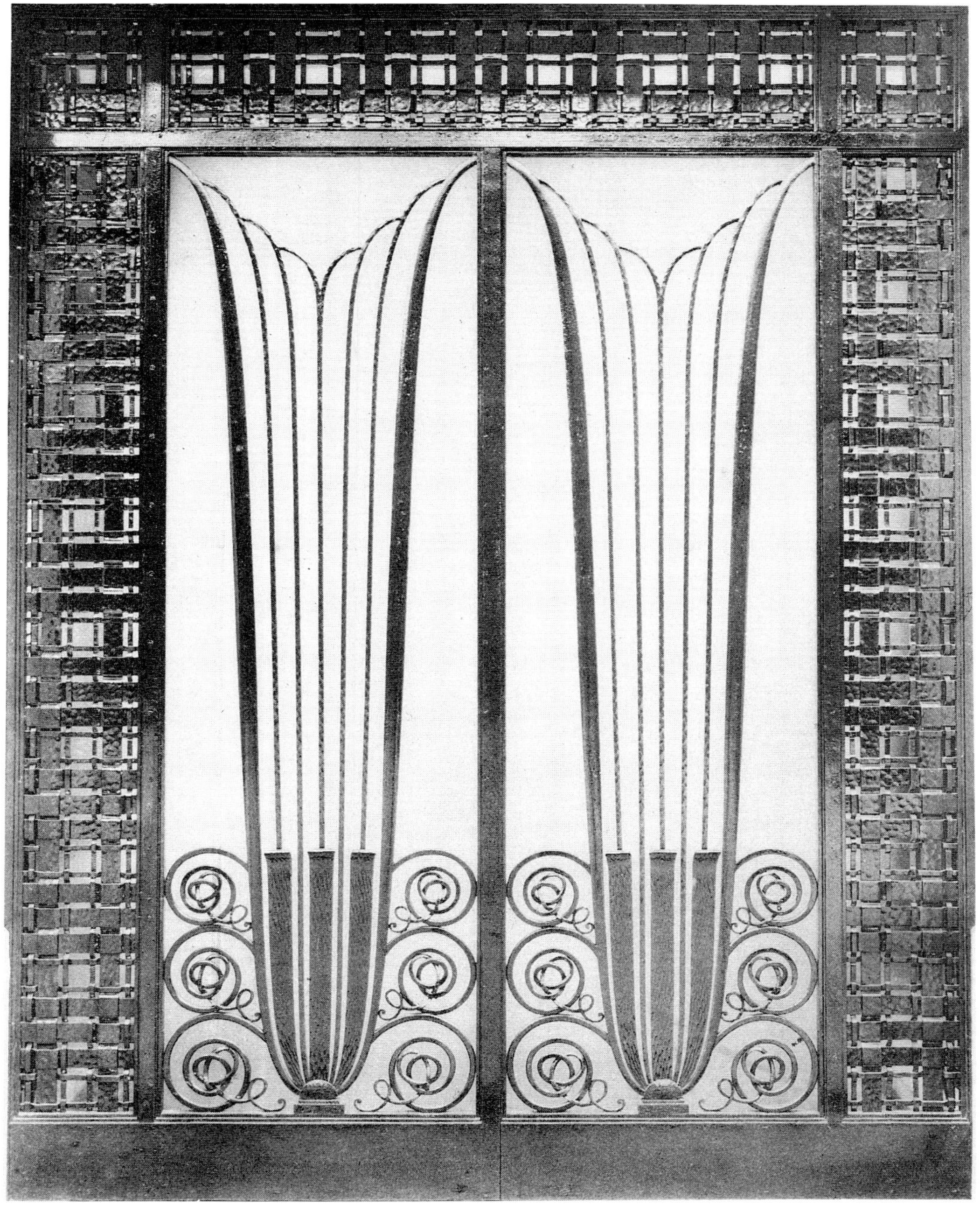

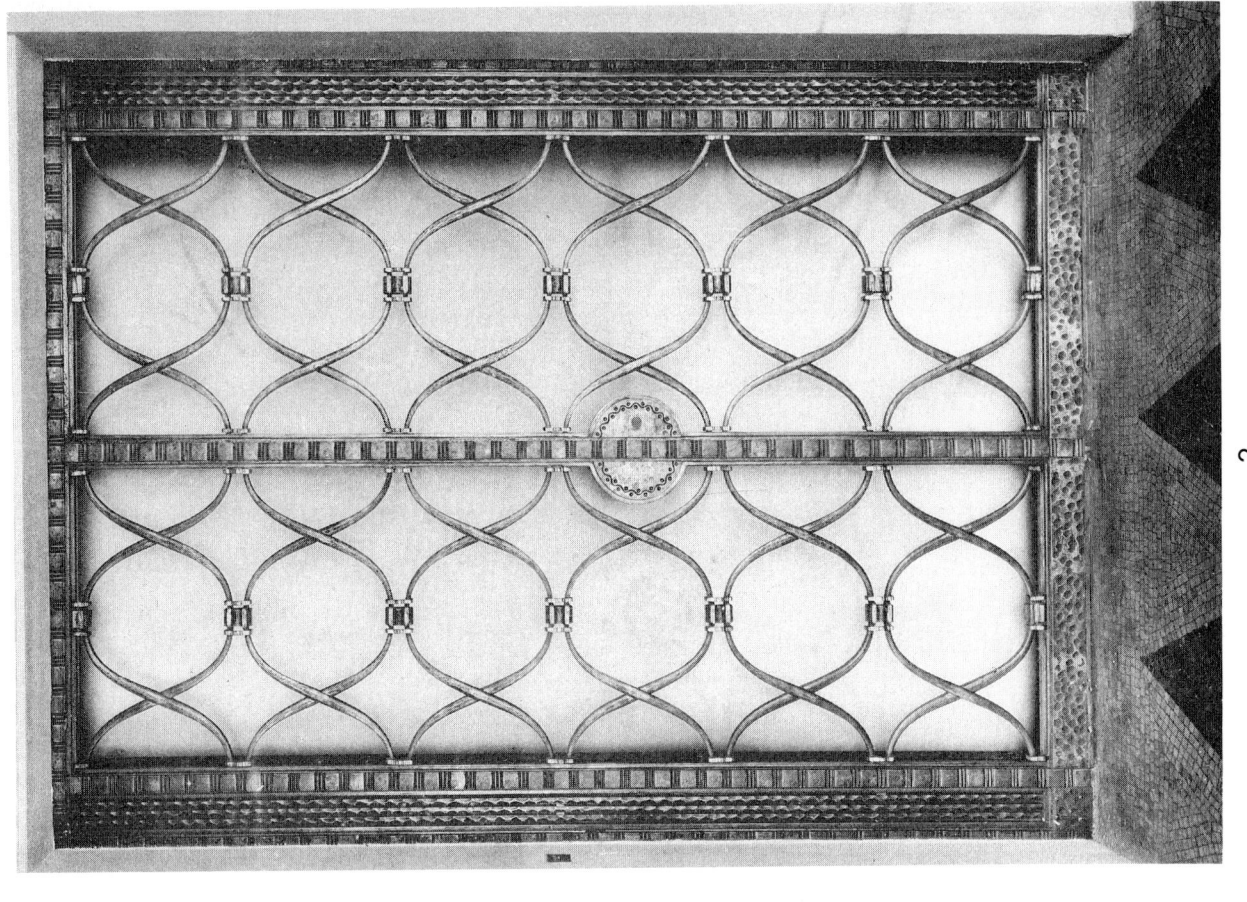

40.　RAYMOND SUBES. (1) Exterior grillwork. (2) Building entrance.

2

1

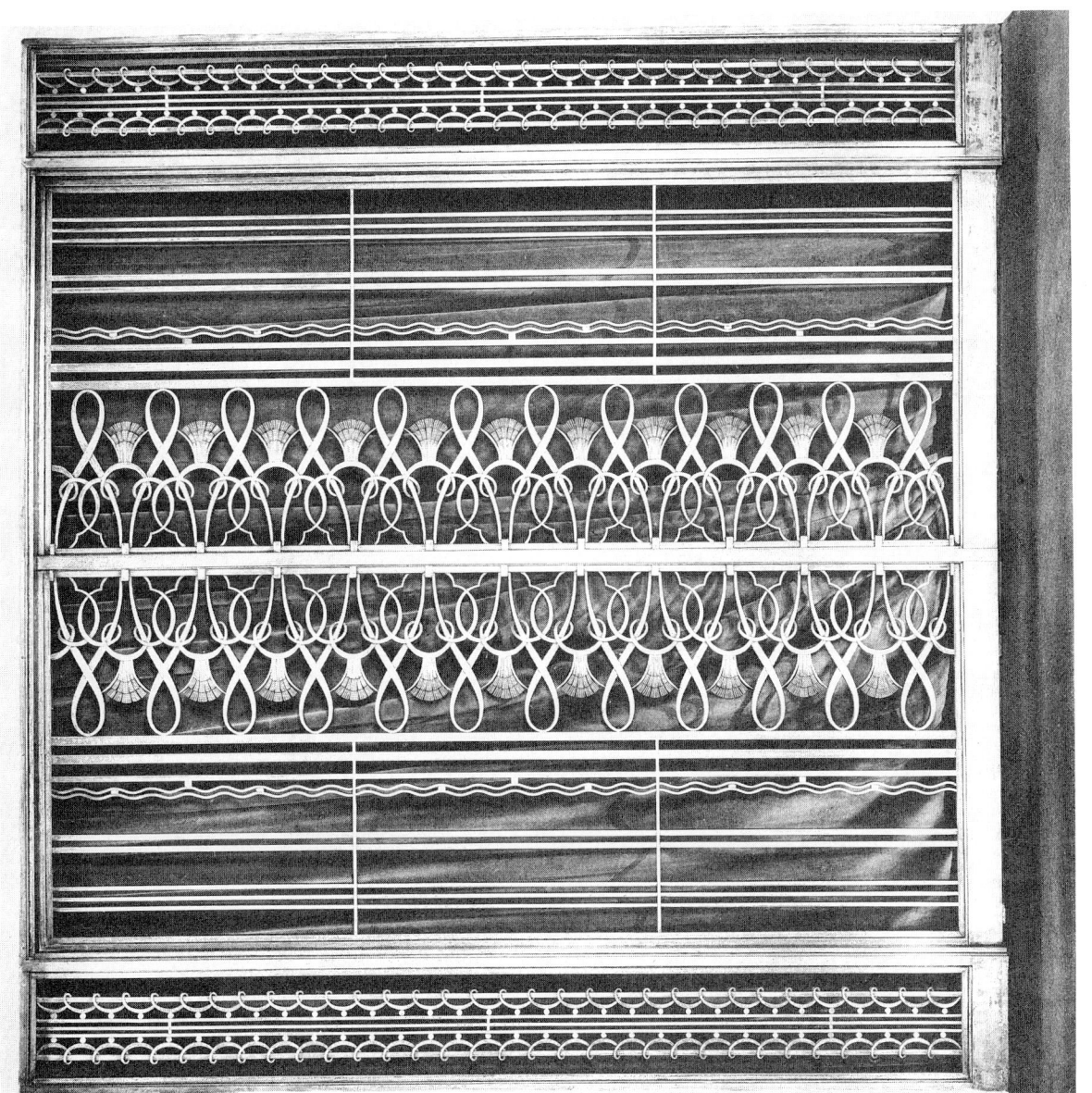

41.   RAYMOND SUBES. (1, 2) Interior grillwork.

1

2

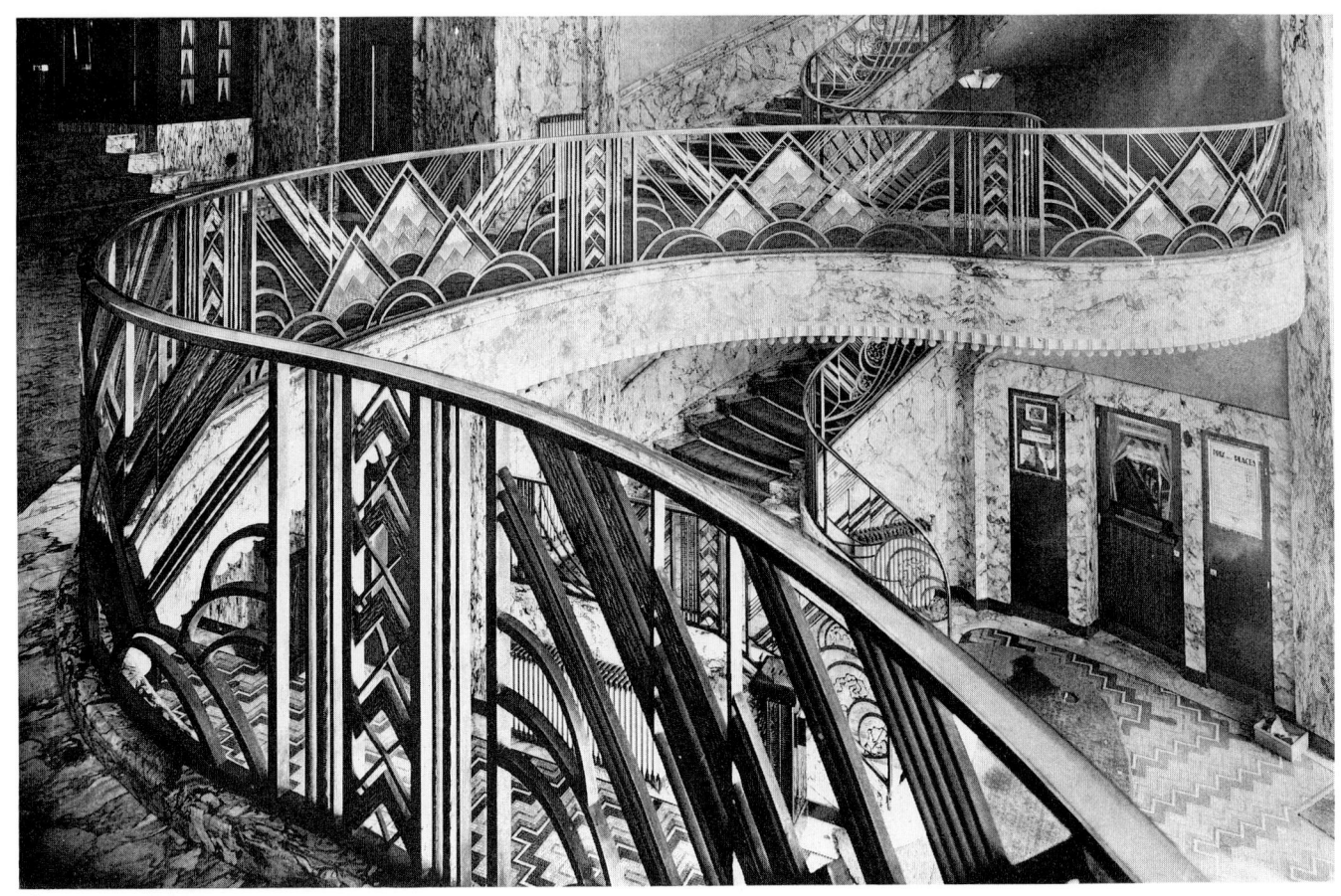

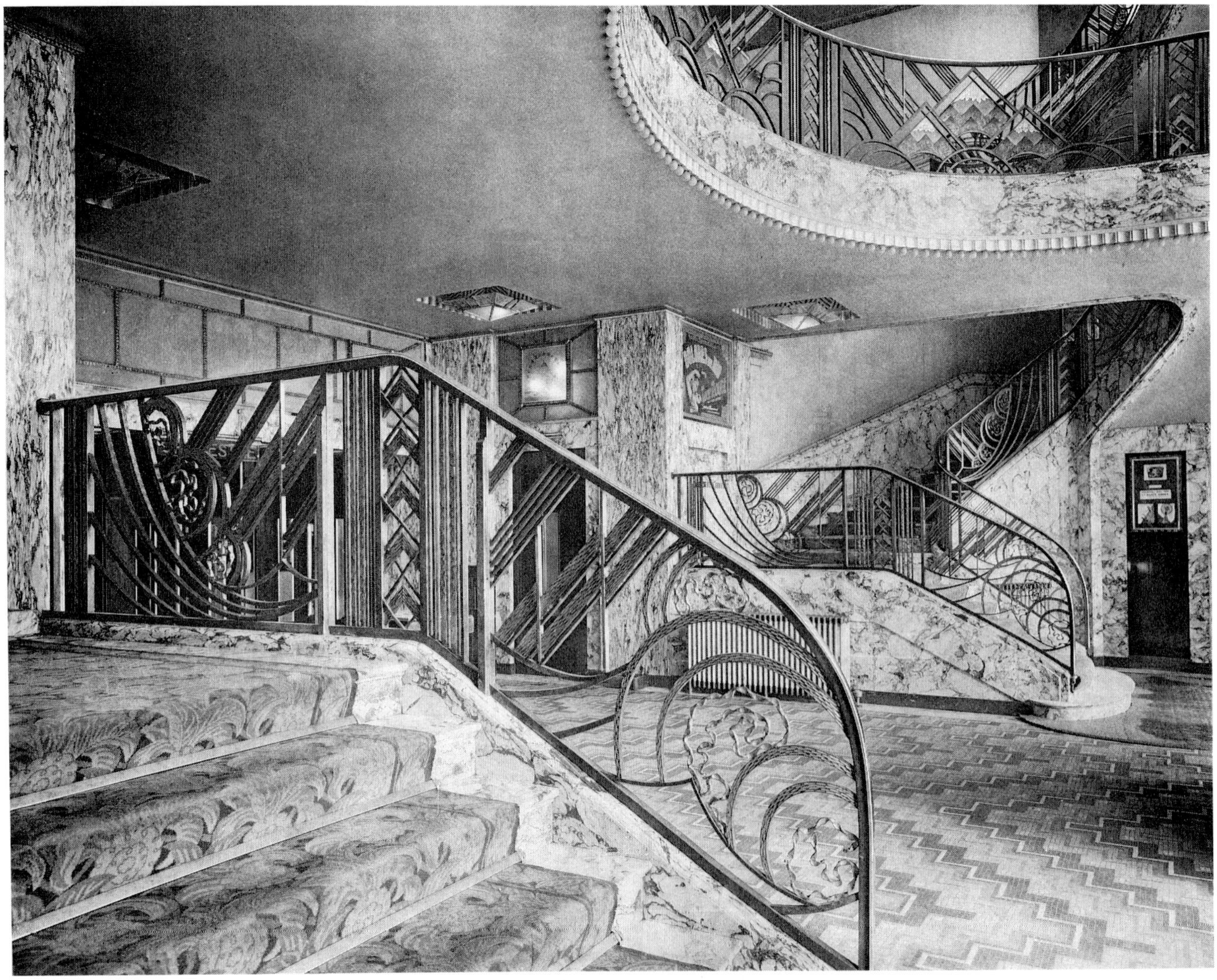

42. Raymond Subes. (1, 2) Balustrade and railings for the Paramount Theatre, Paris.

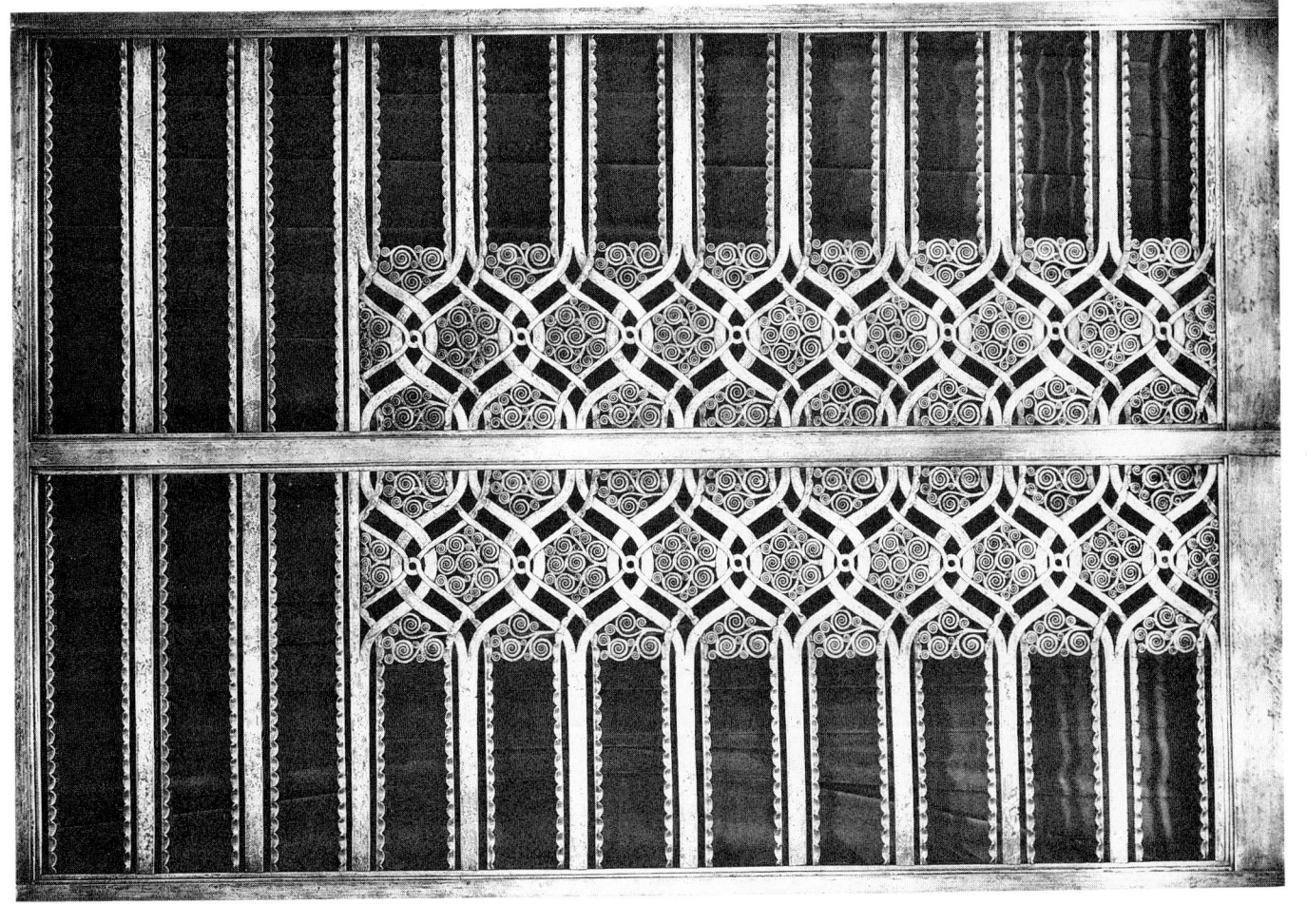

2

1

43.   RAYMOND SUBES. (1) Interior door. (2) Interior grillwork.

1

2

44.   RAYMOND SUBES. (1) Interior grillwork. (2) Mirror and table.

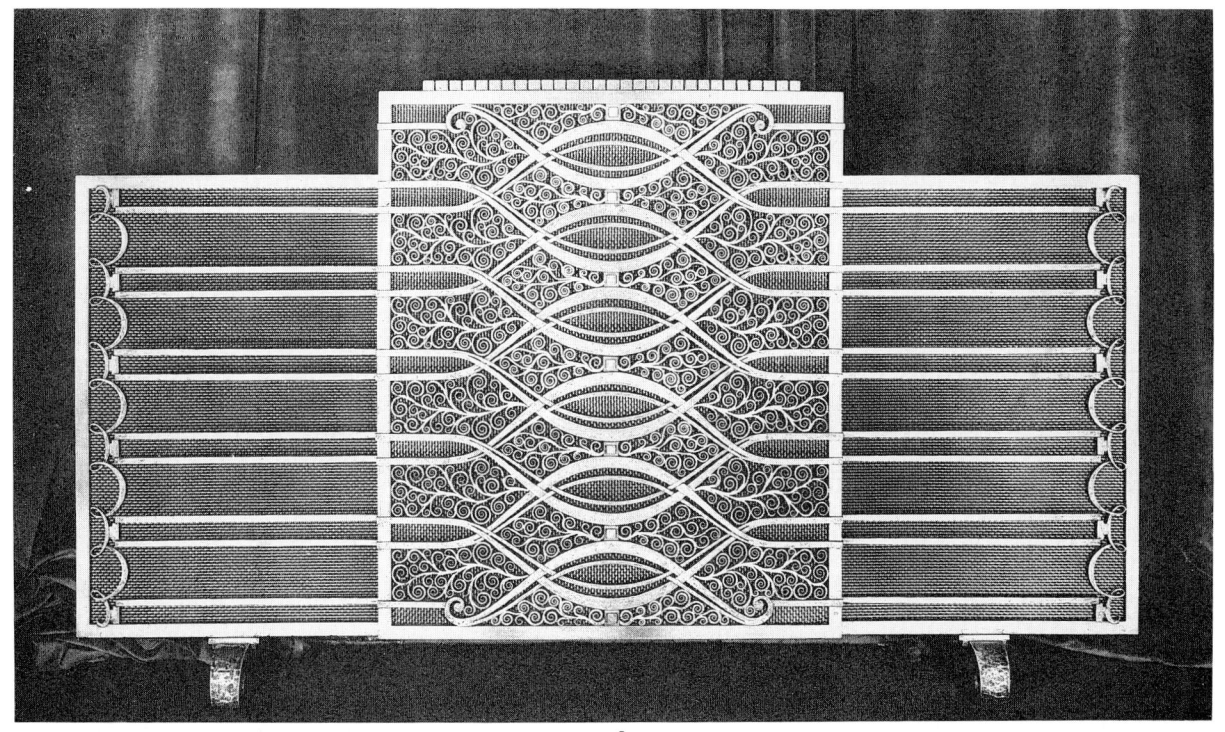

1

2

45.   RAYMOND SUBES. (1) Radiator cover. (2) Grille.

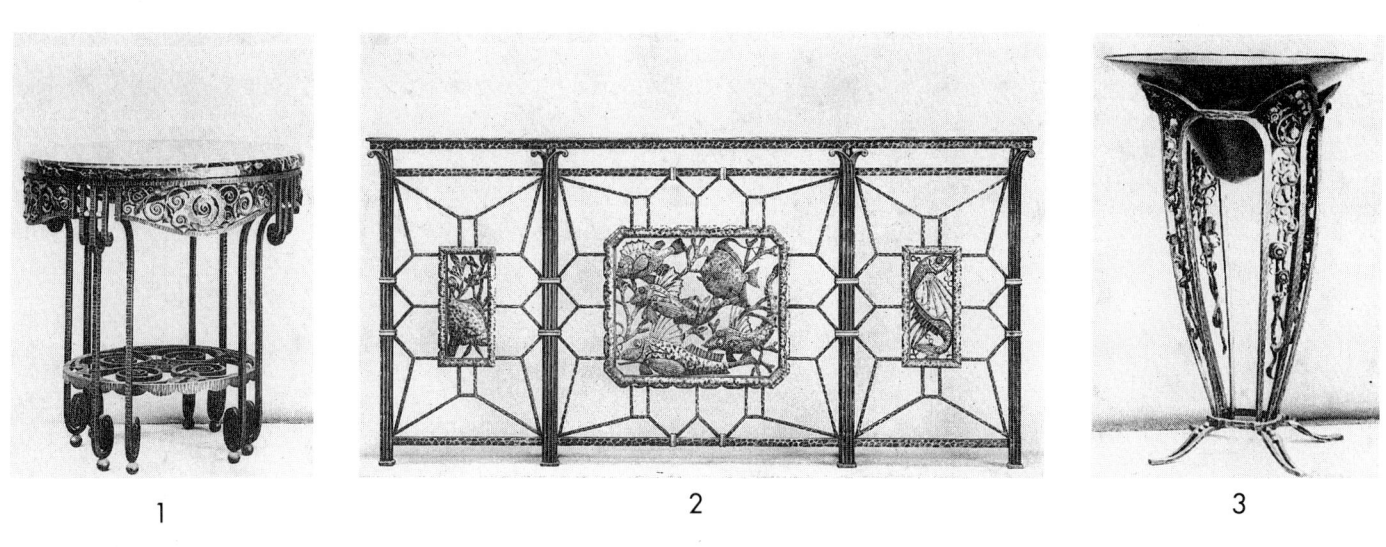

1 2 3

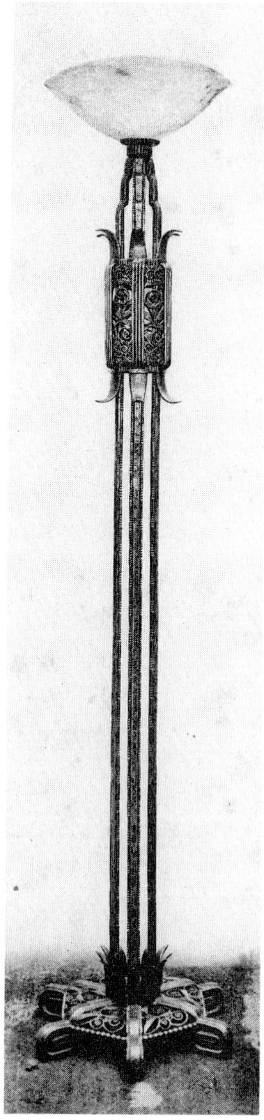

4  5 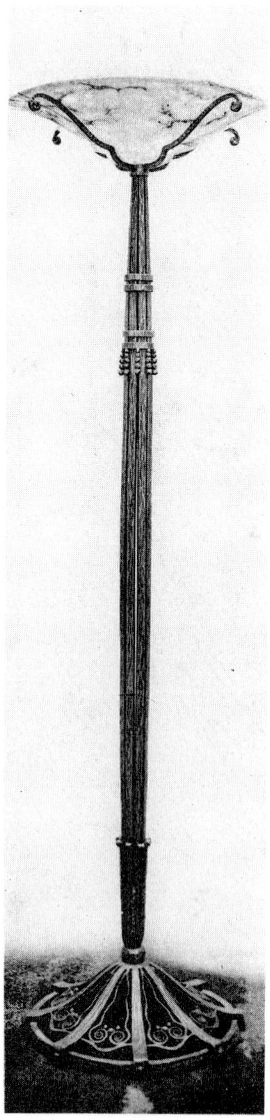 6

46.   GEORGES VINANT. (1) Tea table. (2) Railing. RAYMOND SUBES. (3) Work table. (4) Torchère. MARCEL BERGUE.
(5) Console, mirror, wall sconces, and table lamp. (6) Torchère.

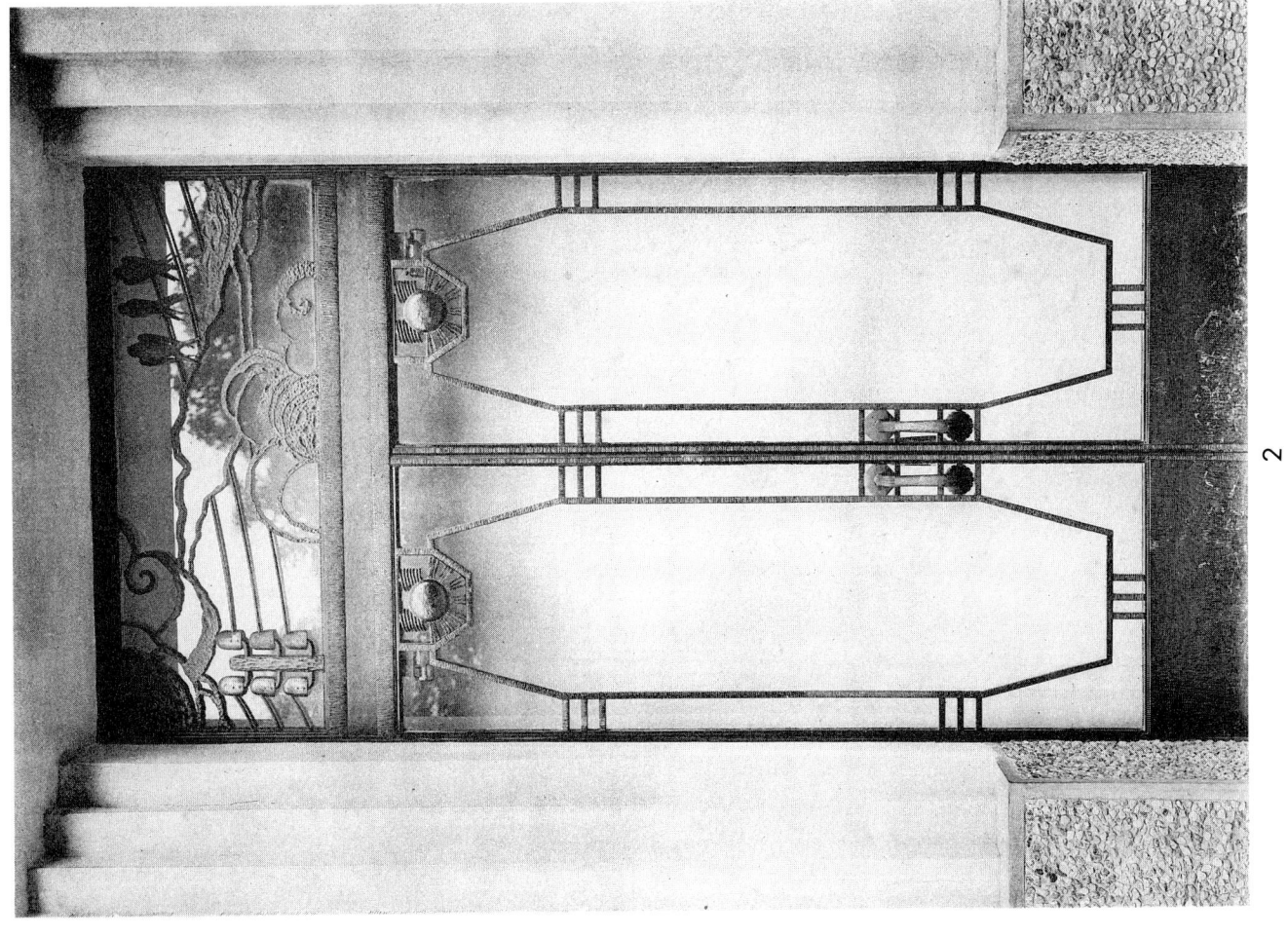

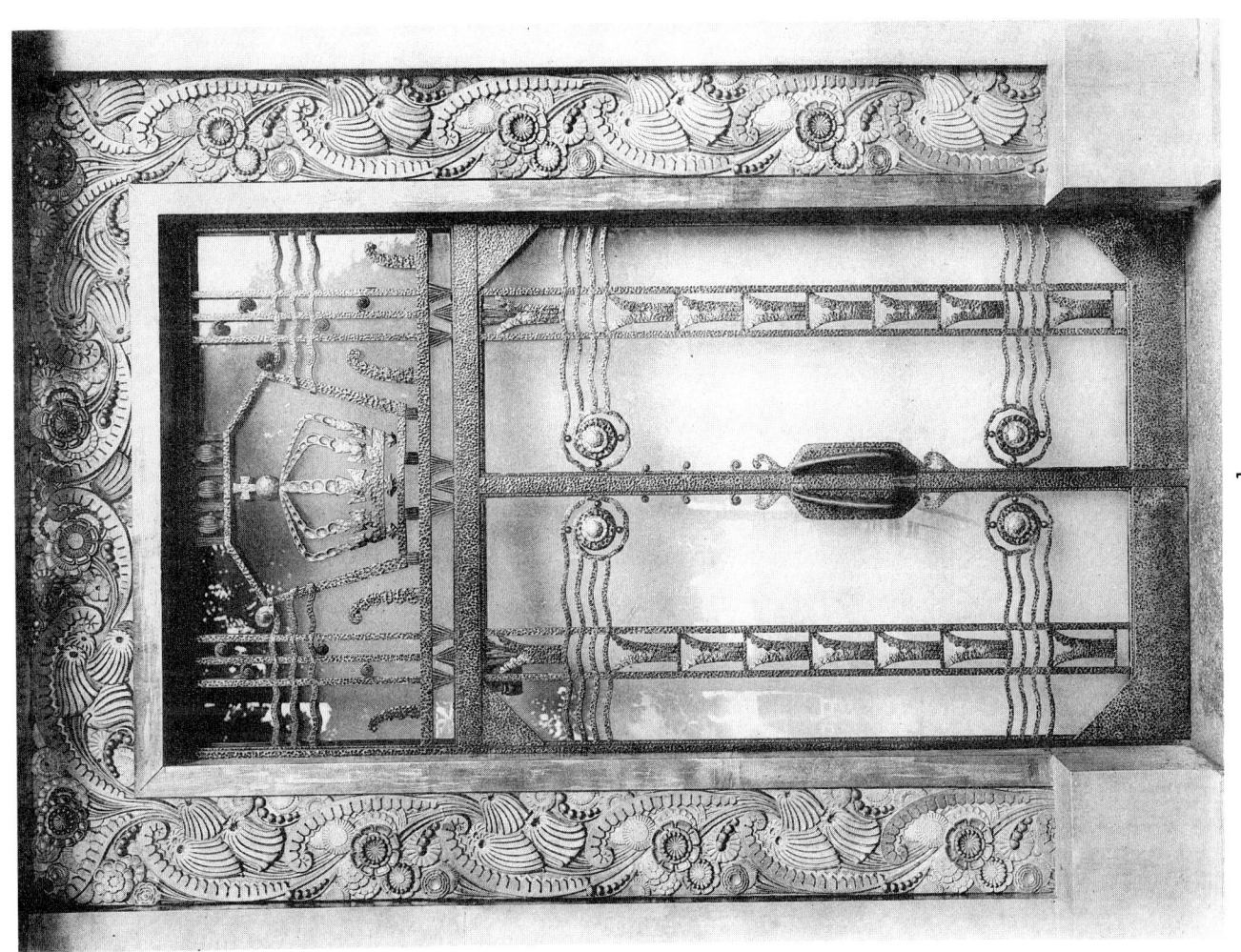

47.　Georges Vinant. (1, 2) Building entrances.

2

1

48.   MARCEL BERGUE. (1, 3, 4) Railings and (2) balcony, Pavillon du Commissariat Général.

49.   MARCEL BERGUE. (1) Chandelier. (2) Railing. (3) Fireplace screen. (4) Console. (5) Table.

2

1

50. MARCEL BERGUE. (1, 2) Radiator covers.

1

2

51. RICHARD DESVALLIÈRES. (1) Interior grillwork, Pavillon de la Cie. des Arts Français. (2) Communion grille.

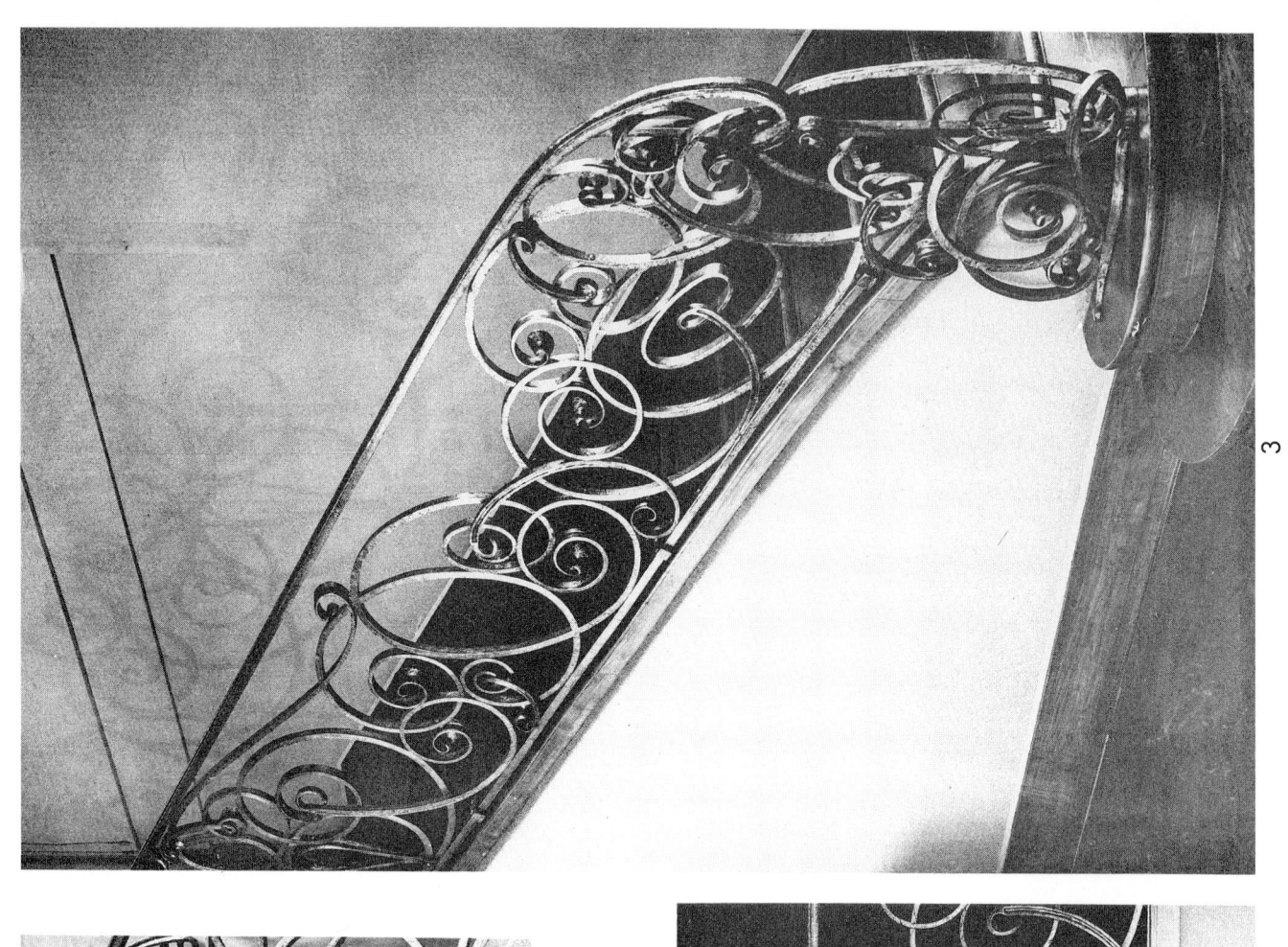

3

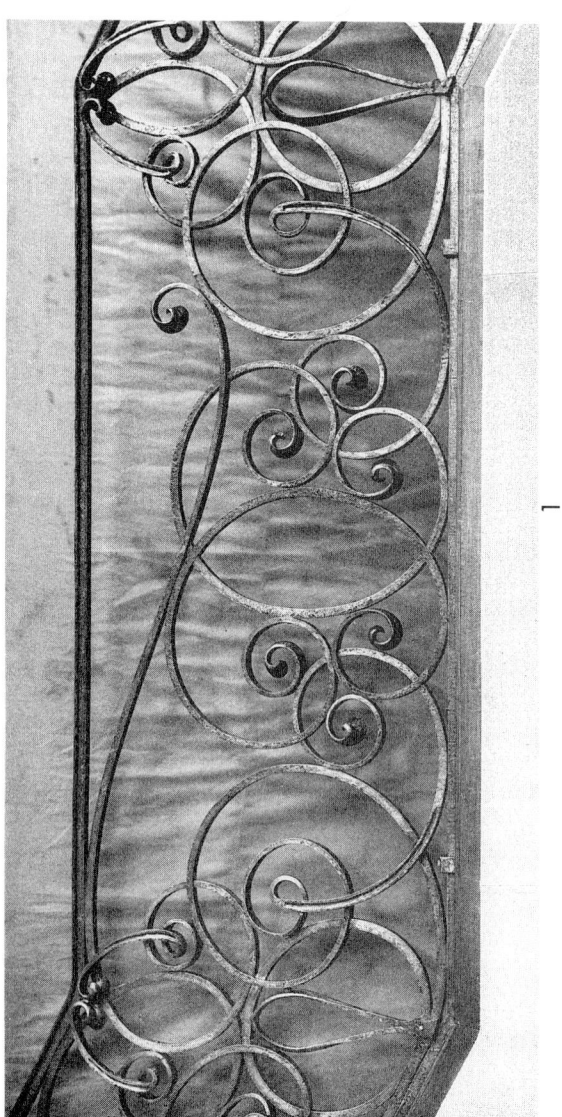

1

2

52. RICHARD DESVALLIÈRES. (1–3) Banisters.

1

2

3

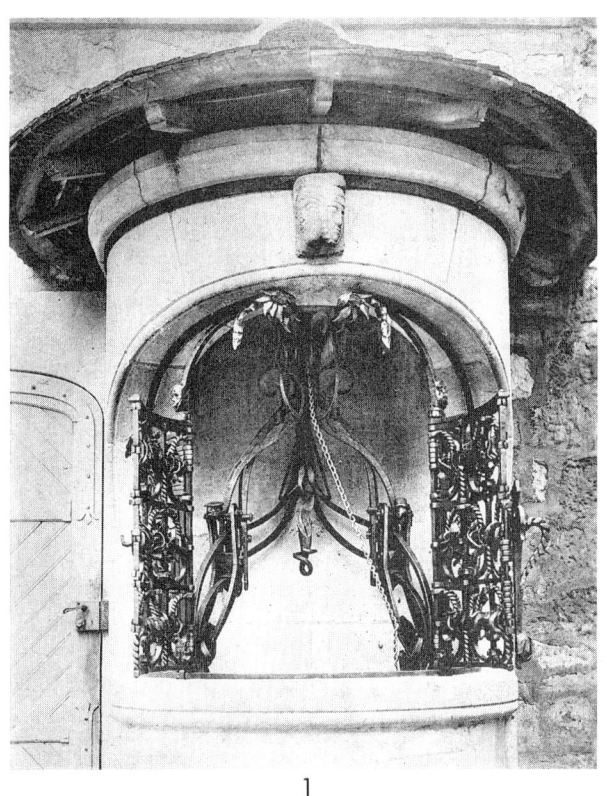

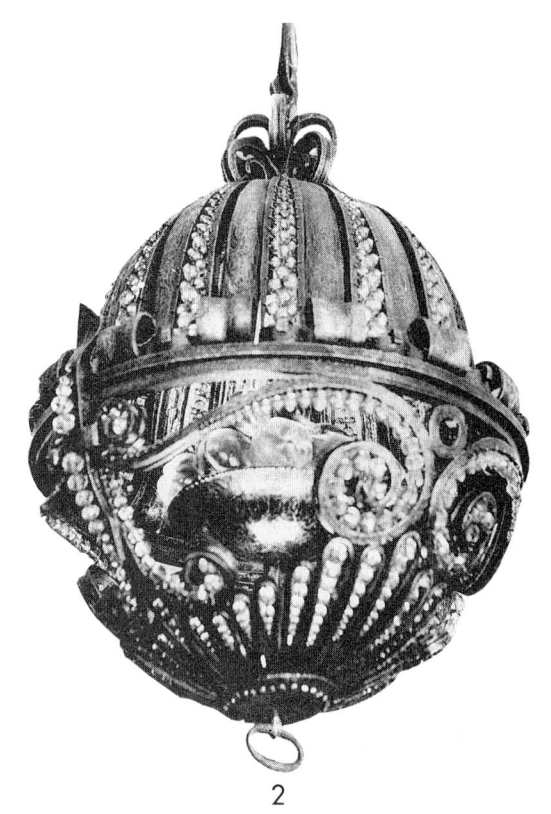

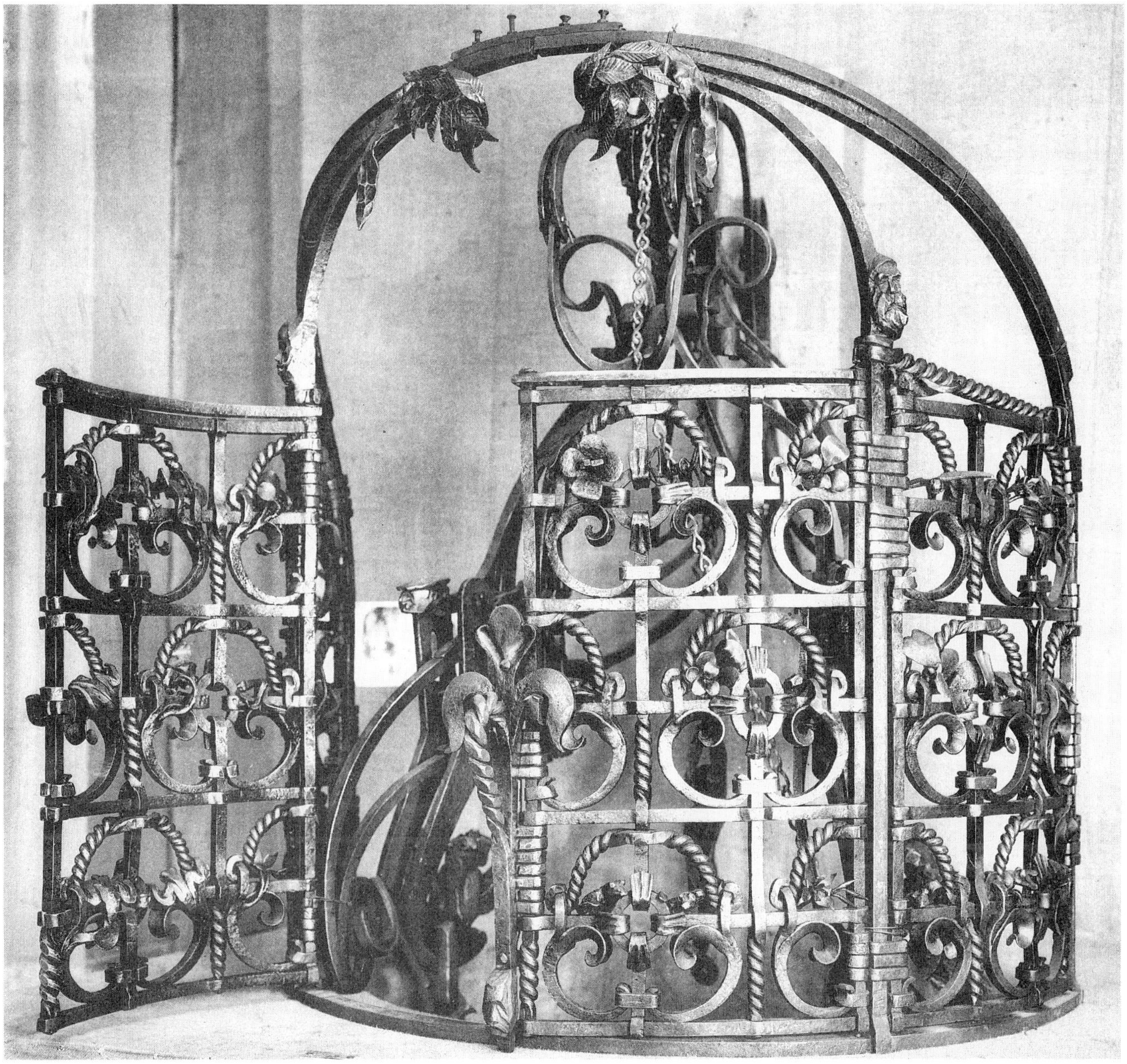

53. Richard Desvallières. (1, 3) Wellhead. (2) Chandelier.

54.   RICHARD DESVALLIÈRES. Console (two views).

1

2

55.   FRED PERRET. (1) Balustrade. (2) Grillwork for an apartment.

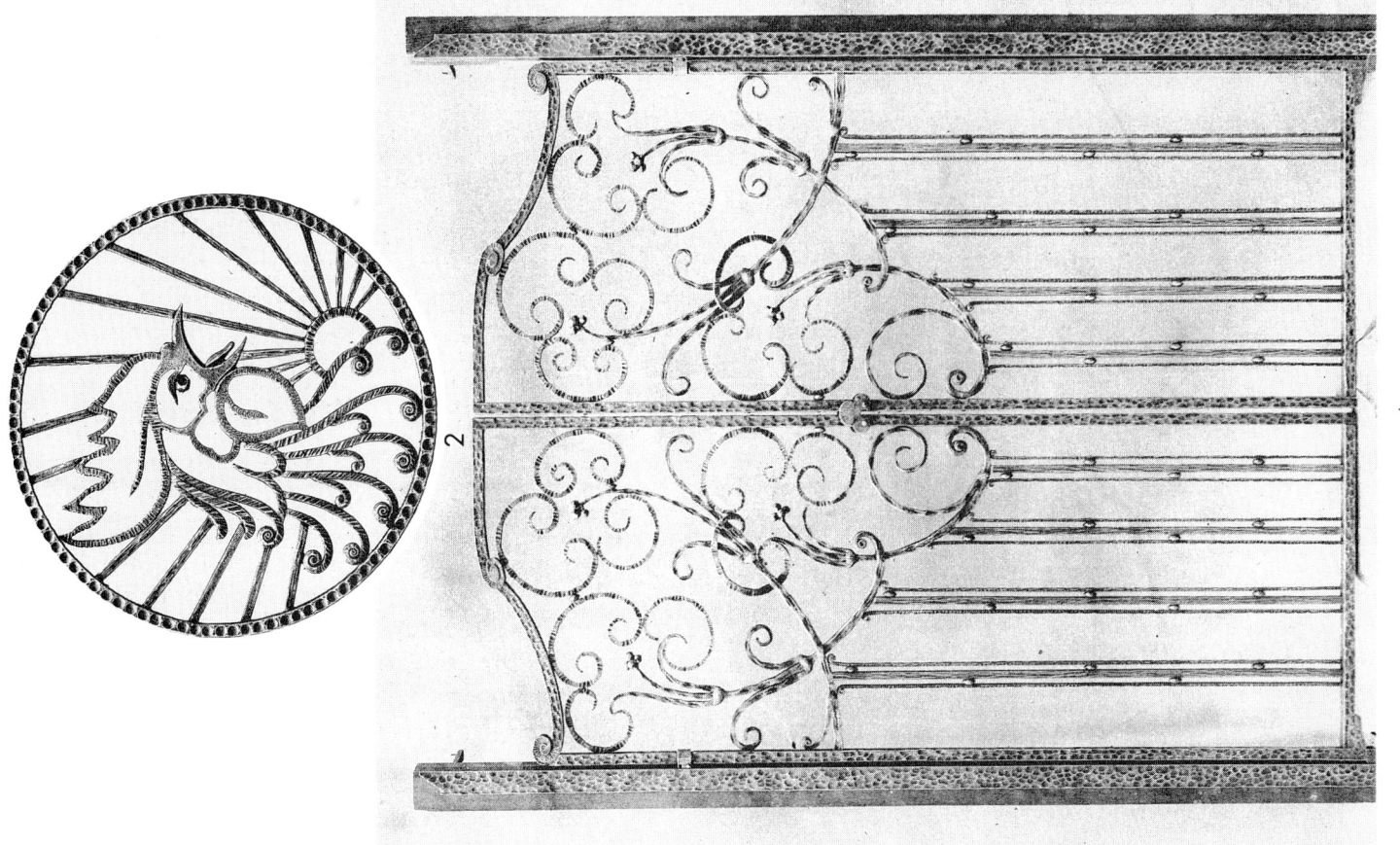

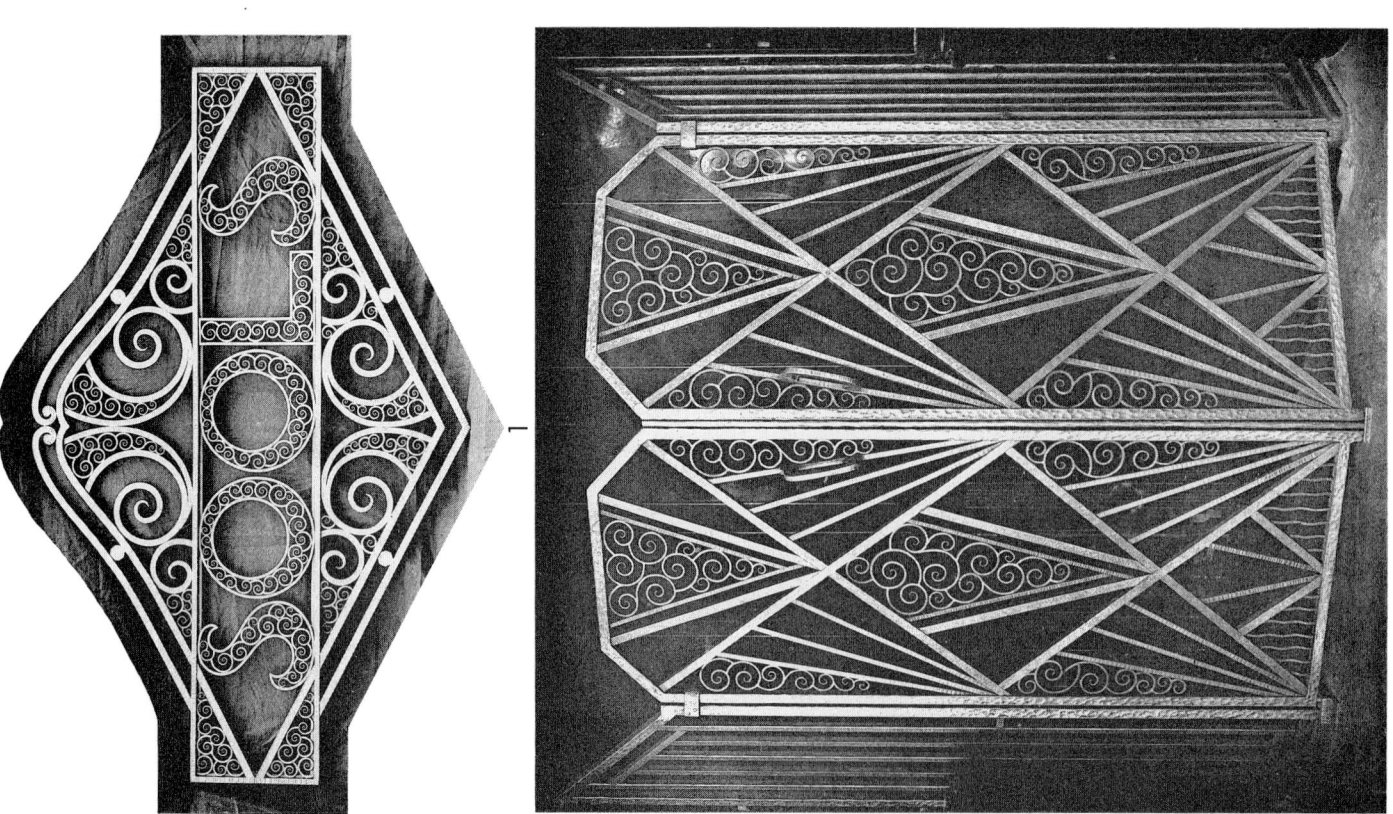

56.   FRED PERRET. (1) Illuminated sign. (2) Table mat. (3, 4) Interior grillwork.

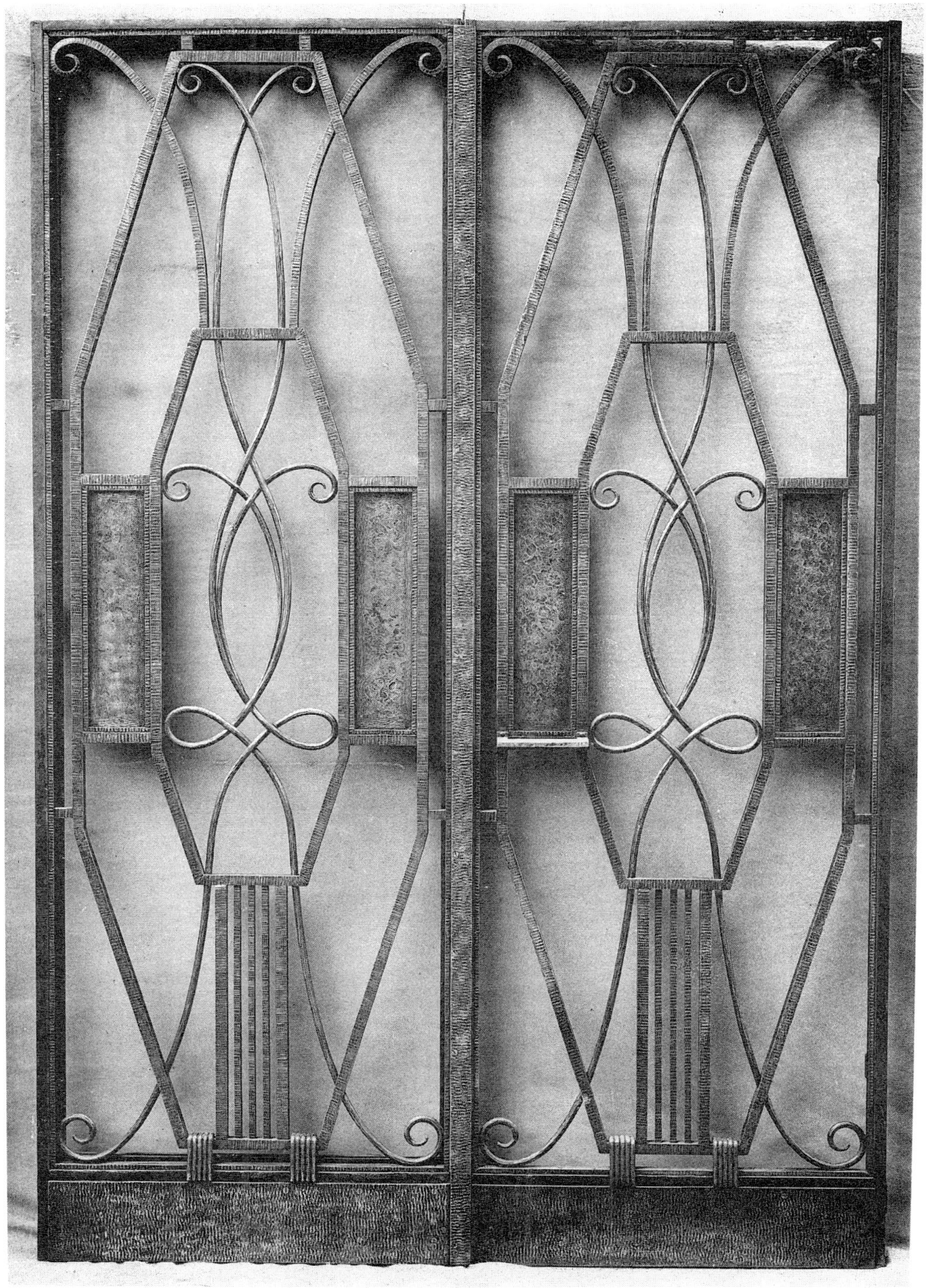

2

1

57.   FRED PERRET. (1) Building entrance. (2) Interior grillwork.

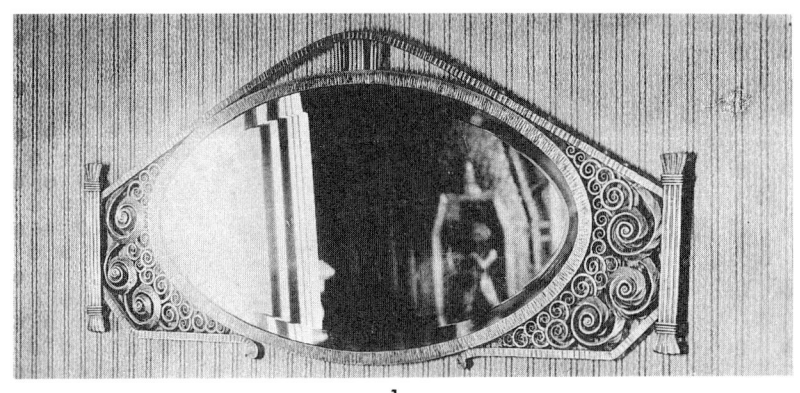

1

2

3

4

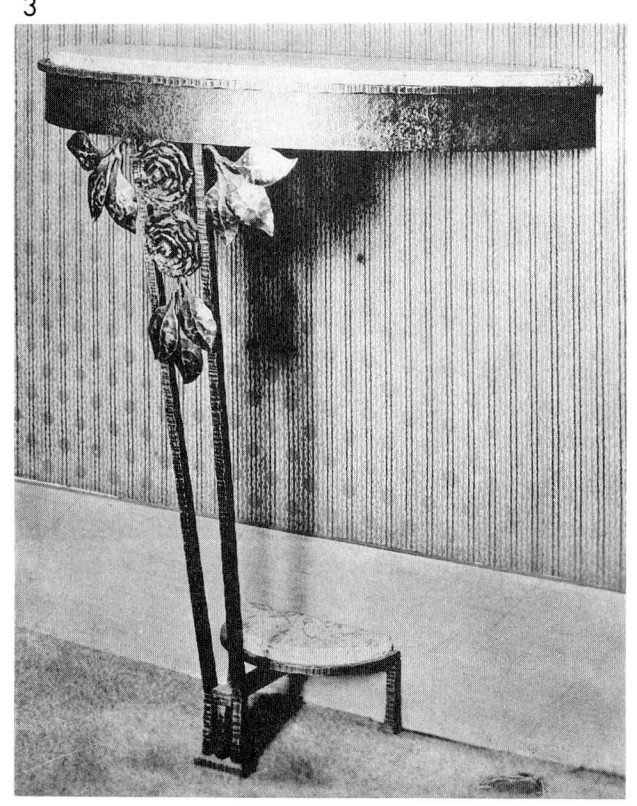

58.   FRED PERRET. (1) Mirror. (2, 4) Consoles. (3) Side table.

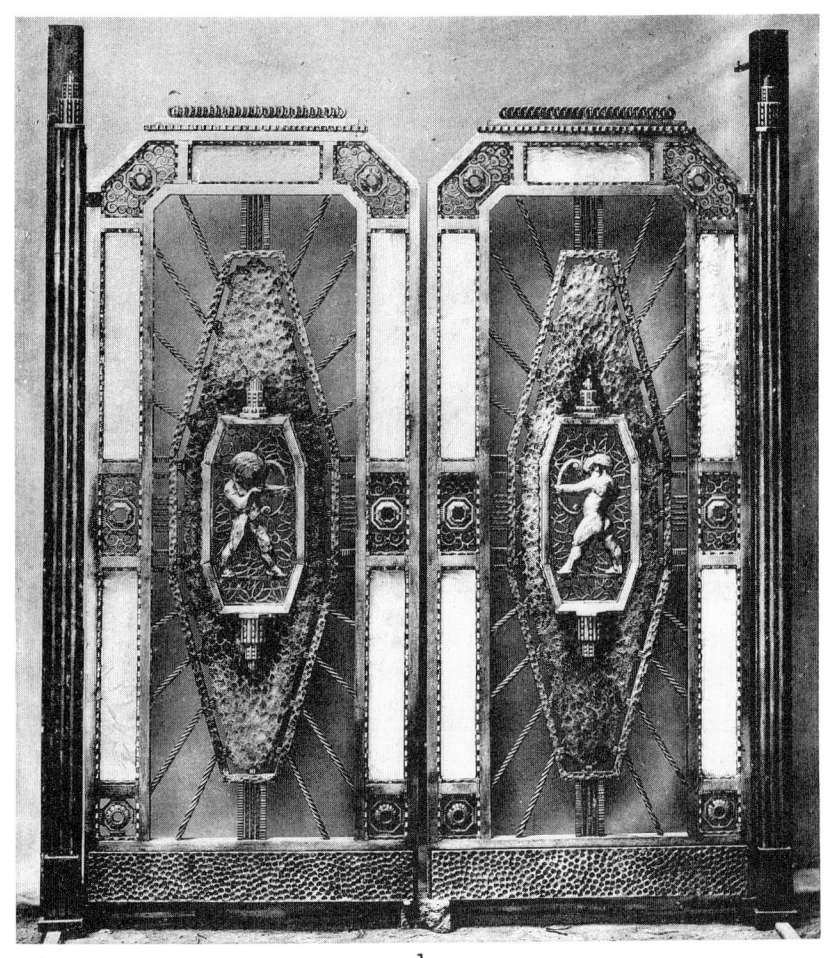

1

2

3

59.   FRED PERRET. (1) Interior door. (2, 3) Interior grillwork.

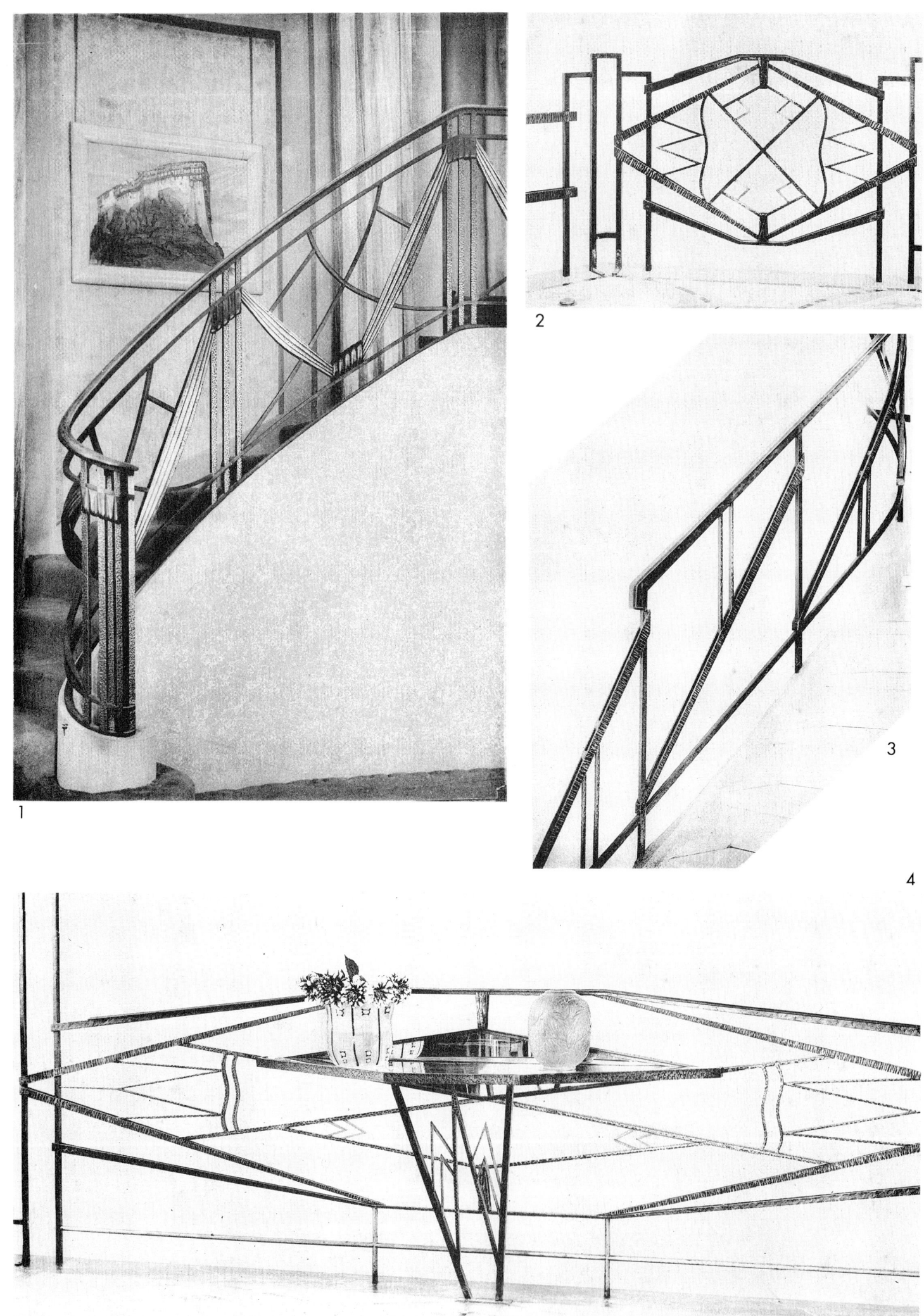

60.   BERNARD. (1) Banister. ETS. SCHWARTZ-HAUTMONT. (2) Grillwork. (3) Banister. (4) Console.

61.   ETS. SCHWARTZ-HAUTMONT. (1) Entrance, Reims library. (2) Entrance, Pavillon Crés et Cie.

62. Ets. Schwartz-Hautmont. (1, 2) Doors for an apartment building.

2

1

1

2

3

63.   ETS. SCHWARTZ-HAUTMONT. (1) Fanlight. (2, 3) Railings.

64.   JEAN SCHWARTZ. (1) Building entrance. (2) Grillwork for an apartment block.

1

2

1

2

65.   JEAN SCHWARTZ. (1) Gate. (2) Railing and grillwork for elevator.

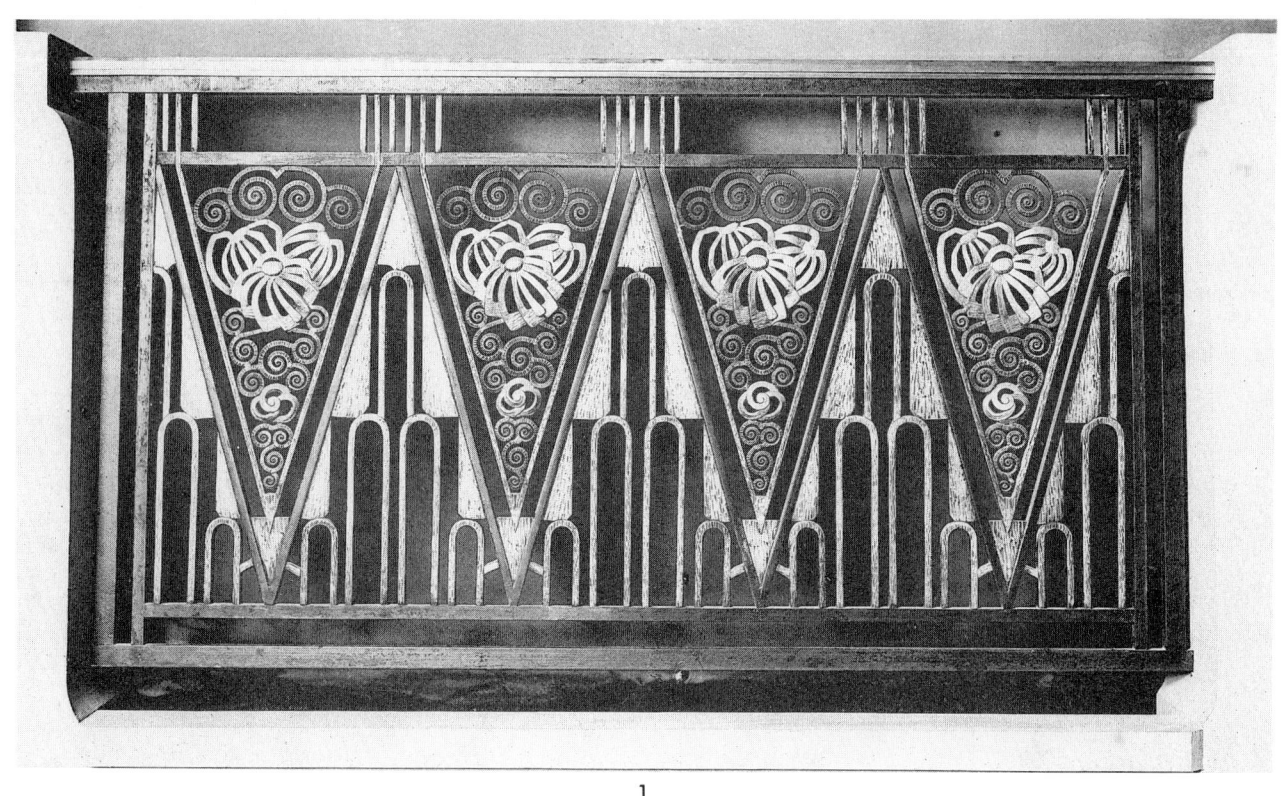

1

2

66.   CHARLES PIGUET. (1) Balcony railing. (2) Entrance, Pavillon de Lyon Saint-Etienne.

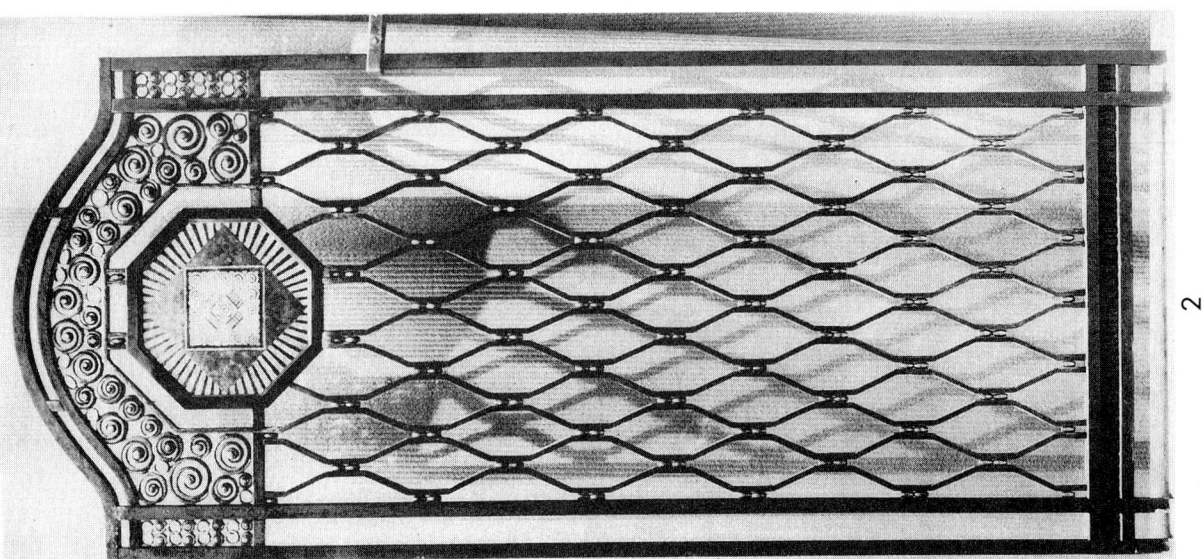

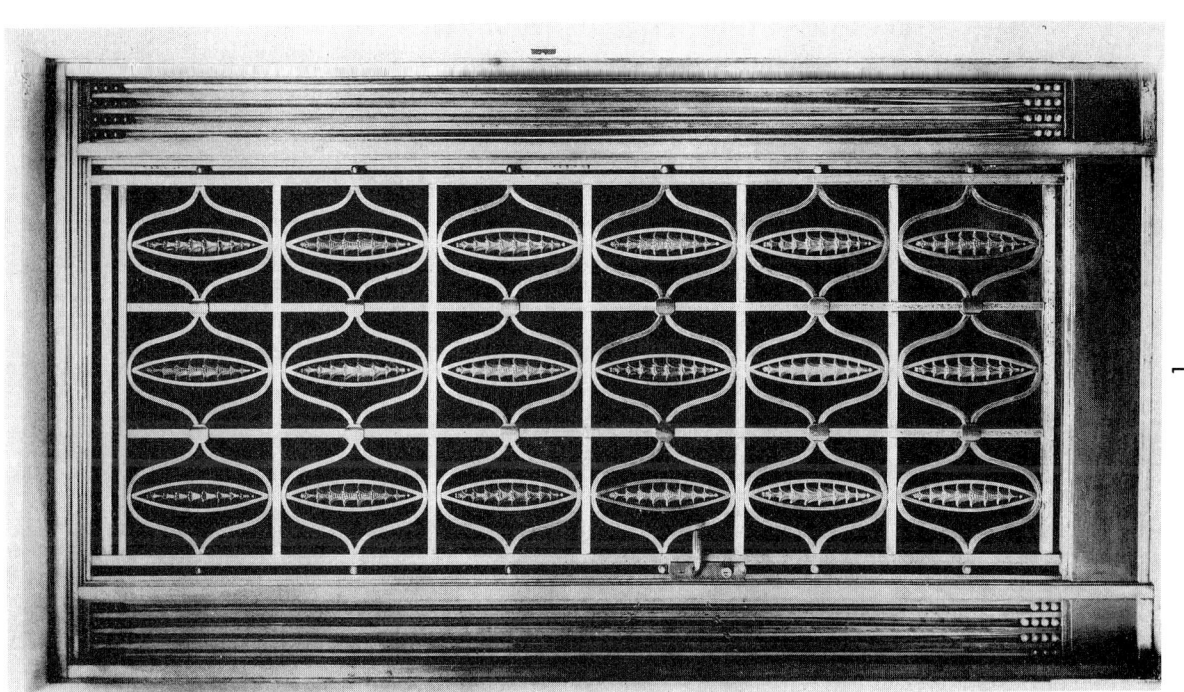

3

2

1

67.   Charles Figuet. (1) Door of polished iron. (2) Elevator grillwork. (3) Building entrance.

68.   CHARLES PIGUET. (1, 2) Radiator covers. (3, 5) Mirrors. (4) Wall sconce. (6) Communion grille.

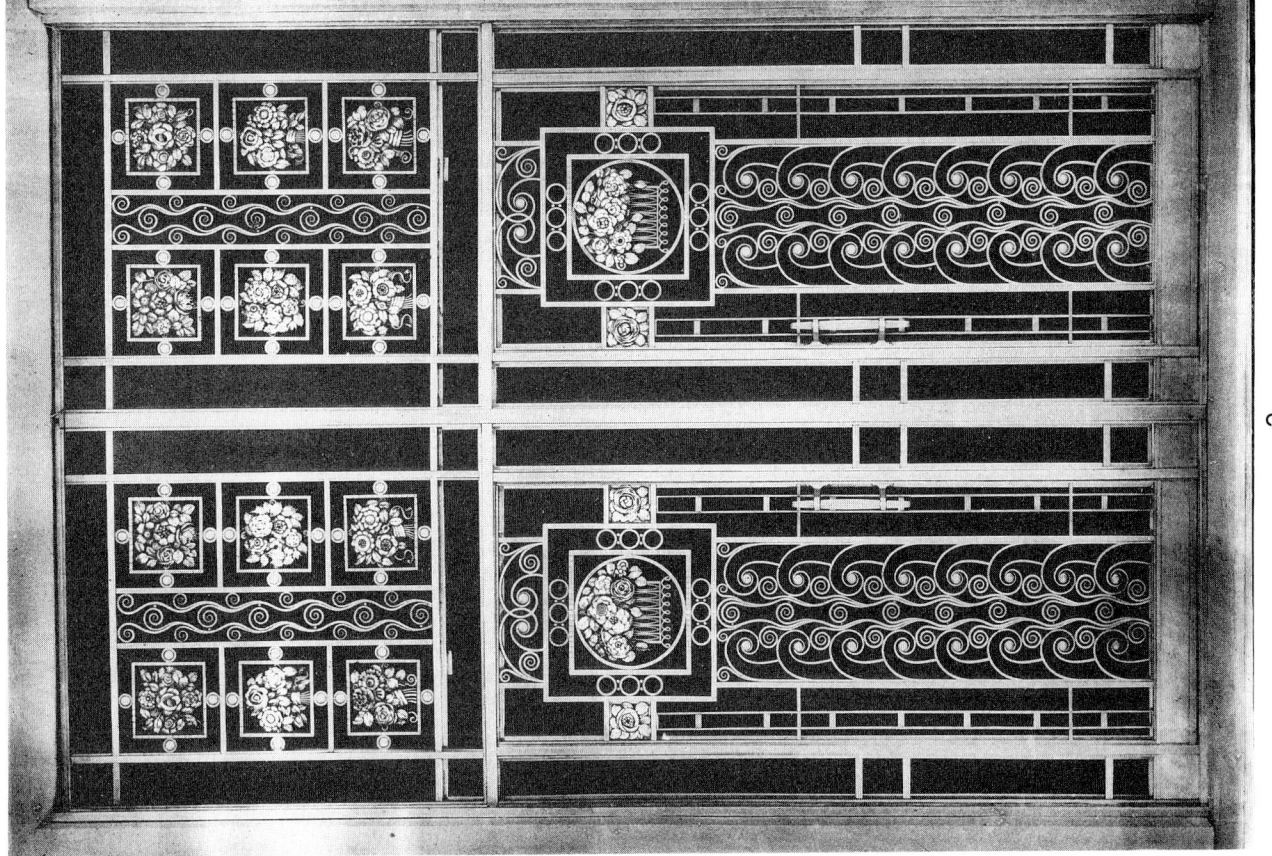

69.   CHARLES PIGUET. (1) Detail and (2) full view of store entrance. (3) Door.

70.   CHARLES PIGUET. (1) Console. (2) Radiator cover. (3) Gate. (4) Hall stand.

2

1

71.   E. Schenck et ses Fils. (1) Building entrance. (2) Entrance to an office building.

72. E. Schenck et ses Fils. (1) Entrance and (2) exit, Pavillon Arthur Goldsheider.

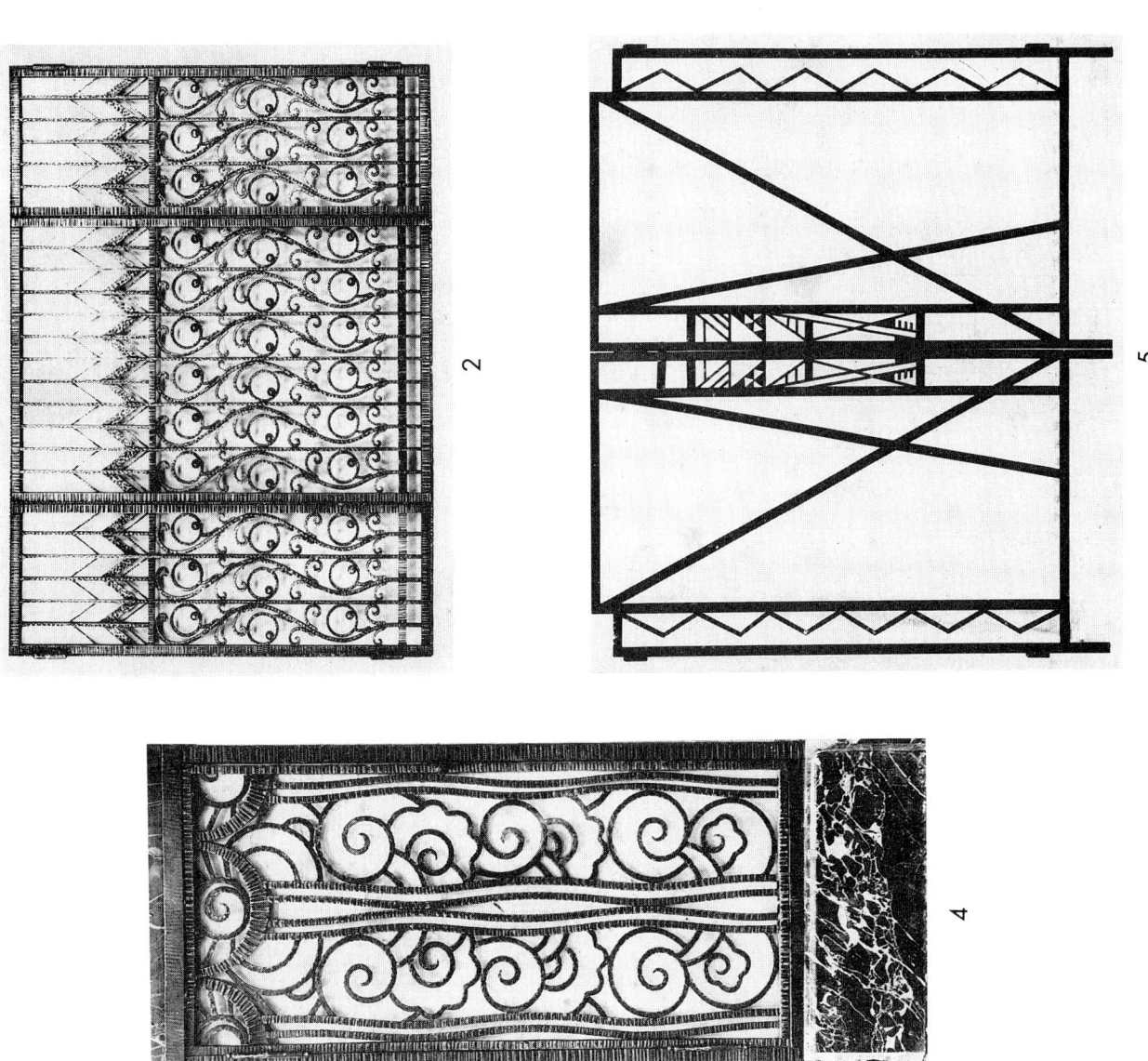

73. E. SCHENCK ET SES FILS. (1, 2, 4) Radiator covers. (3, 5) Grilles.

74.   E. SCHENCK ET SES FILS. (1, 4) Balconies. (2, 3) Interior balconies.

75.　E. Schenck et ses Fils. (1, 2) Banisters.

2

1

1

2

3

76.   E. Schenck et ses Fils. (1) Console desserte. (2) Grille. (3) Interior grillwork.

77. EDOUARD SCHENCK. (1, 2) Banisters. (3) Building entrance.

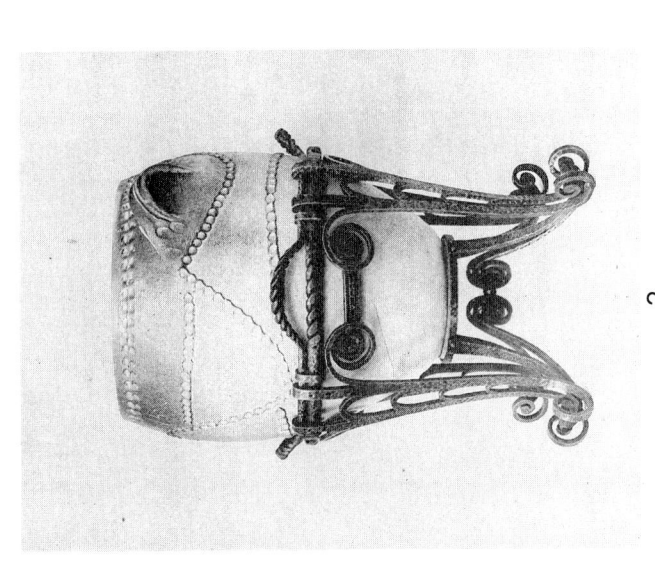

2

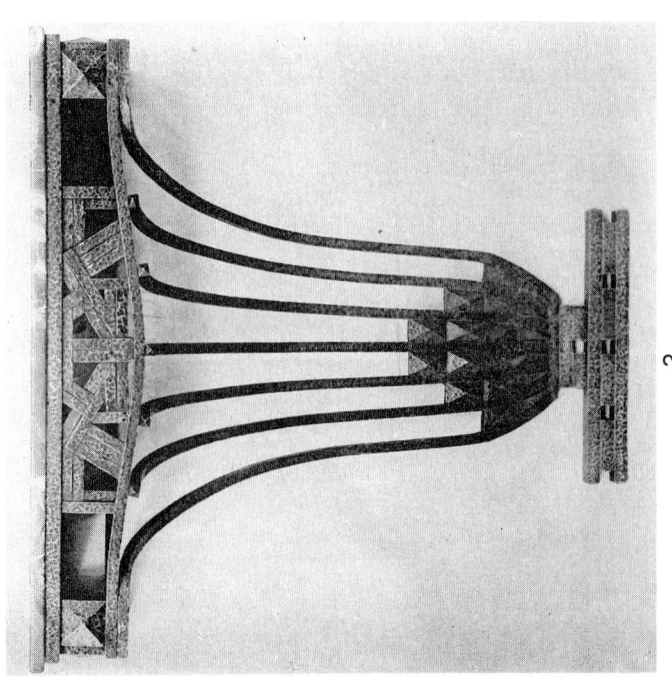

5

4

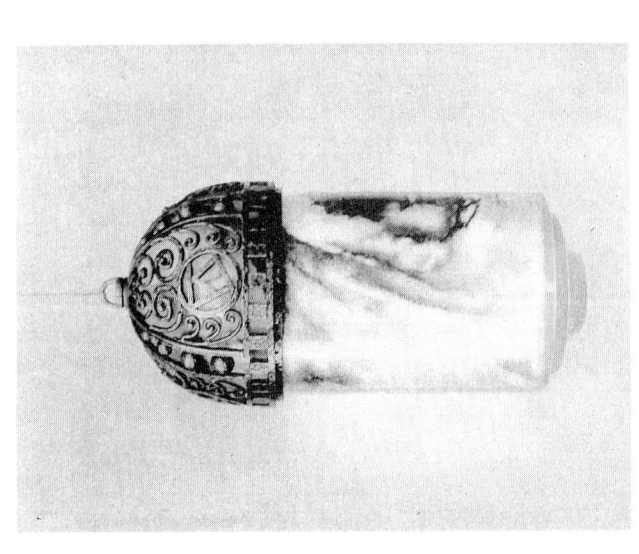

1

3

78.   EDOUARD SCHENCK. (1) Lantern. (3) Console. CHARLES SCHENCK. (5) Interior grillwork. MARCEL SCHENCK. (2) Ironwork stand for a vase. (4) Radiator cover.

1

2

79.   EDOUARD SCHENCK. (1) Interior grillwork. MARCEL SCHENCK. (2) Carriage gate.

1   2

3   4

5

80.   EDOUARD SCHENCK. (1, 2) Interior grillwork. (3, 4) Radiator covers. (5) Grillwork for the luxury liner
"Ile de France."

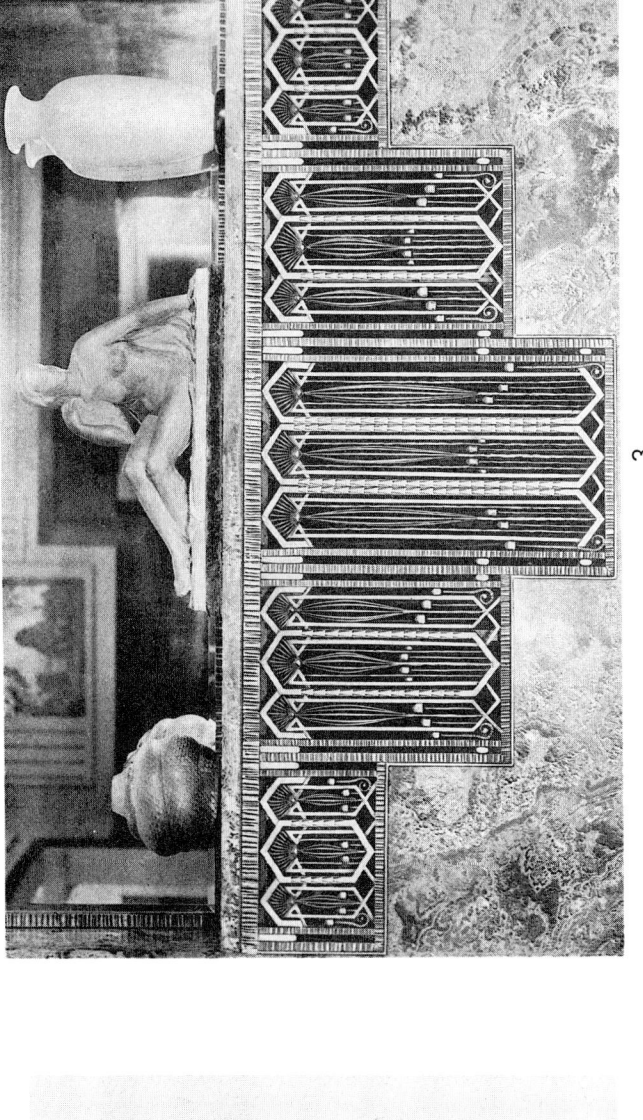

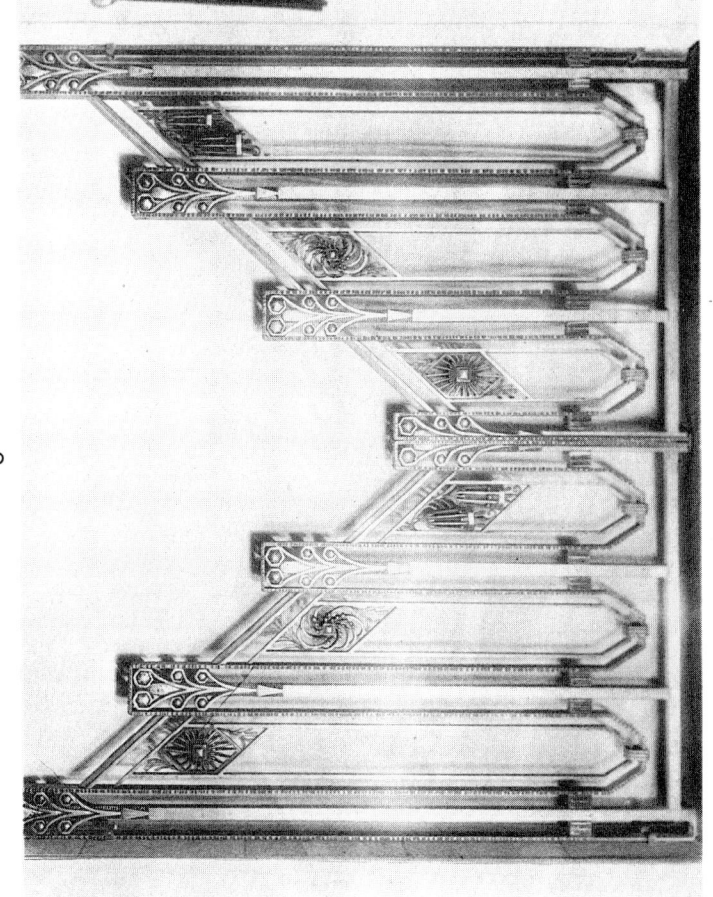

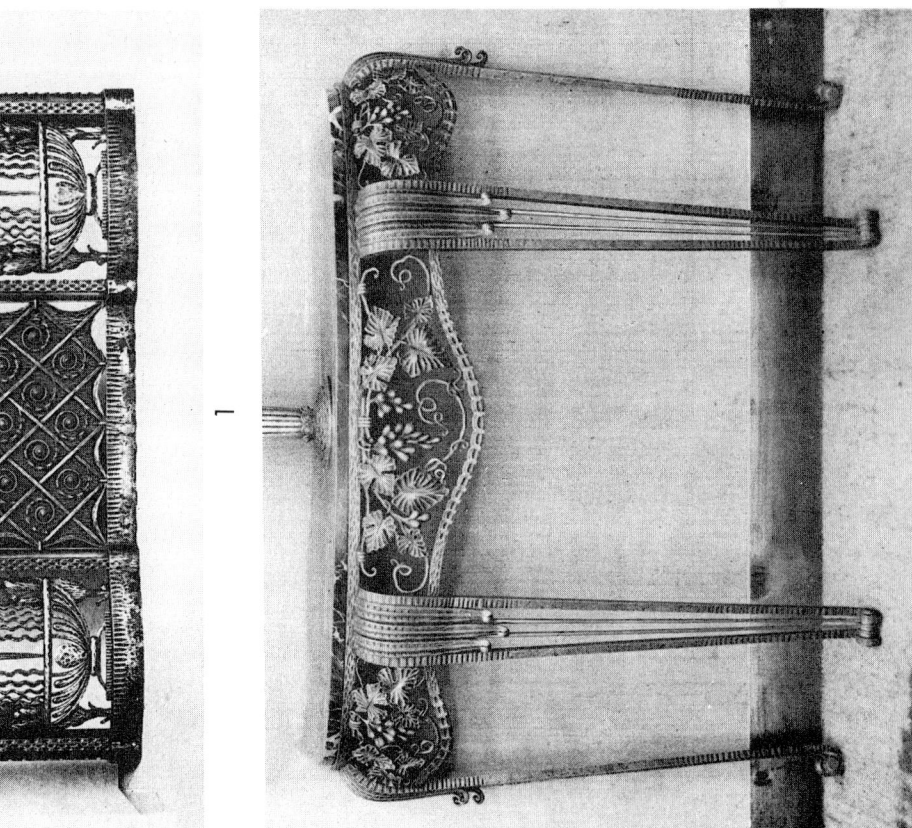

3

4

1

2

81.   MALATRE AND TONNELLIER. (1) Radiator cover. (2) Console. MAJORELLE FRÈRES. (3) Mantelpiece. (4) Grille.

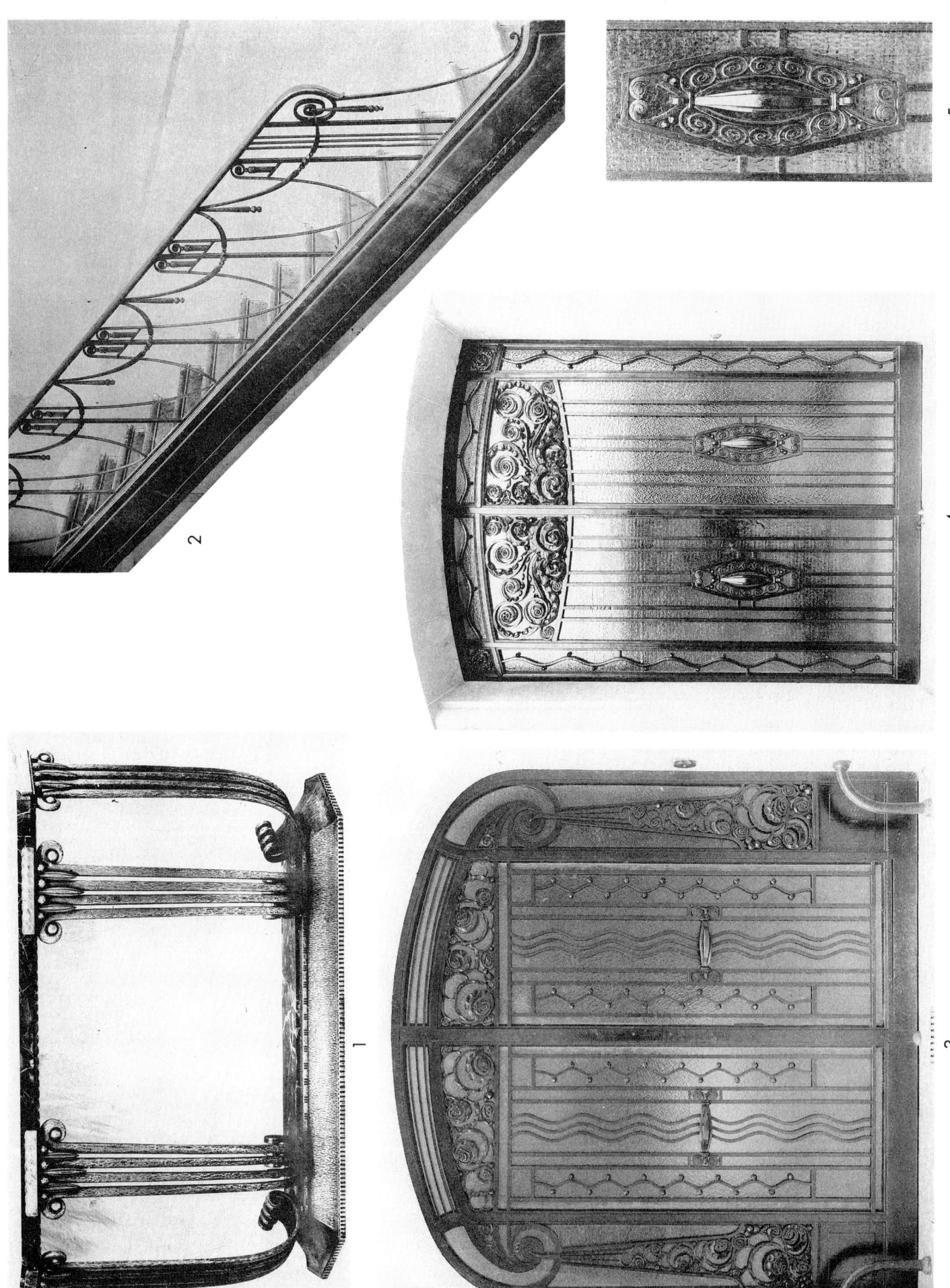

82. MALATRE AND TONNELLIER. (1) Console. (2) Banister. (3, 4) Entrance grilles. (5) Door handle (detail).

2

1

83.   Raingo Frères. (1) Storefront, Tétard Frères. Nics Frères. (2) Storefront, Alexandre.

84. Nics Frères. (1, 2) Chandeliers. (3, 5, 7) Torchères. (4) Wall sconce. (6) Candelabrum.

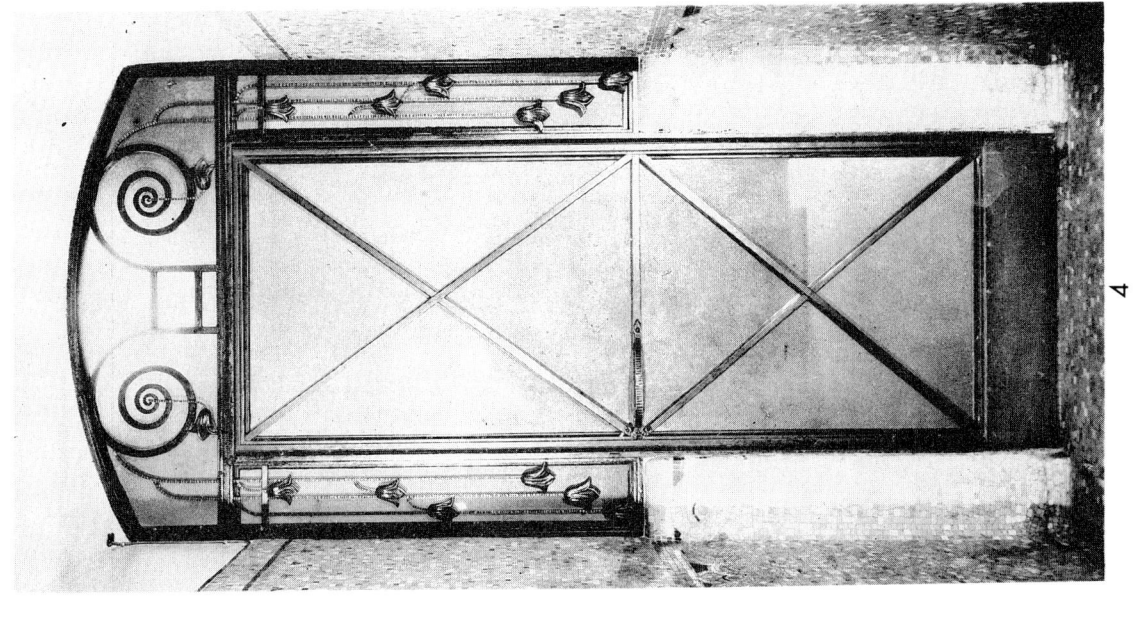

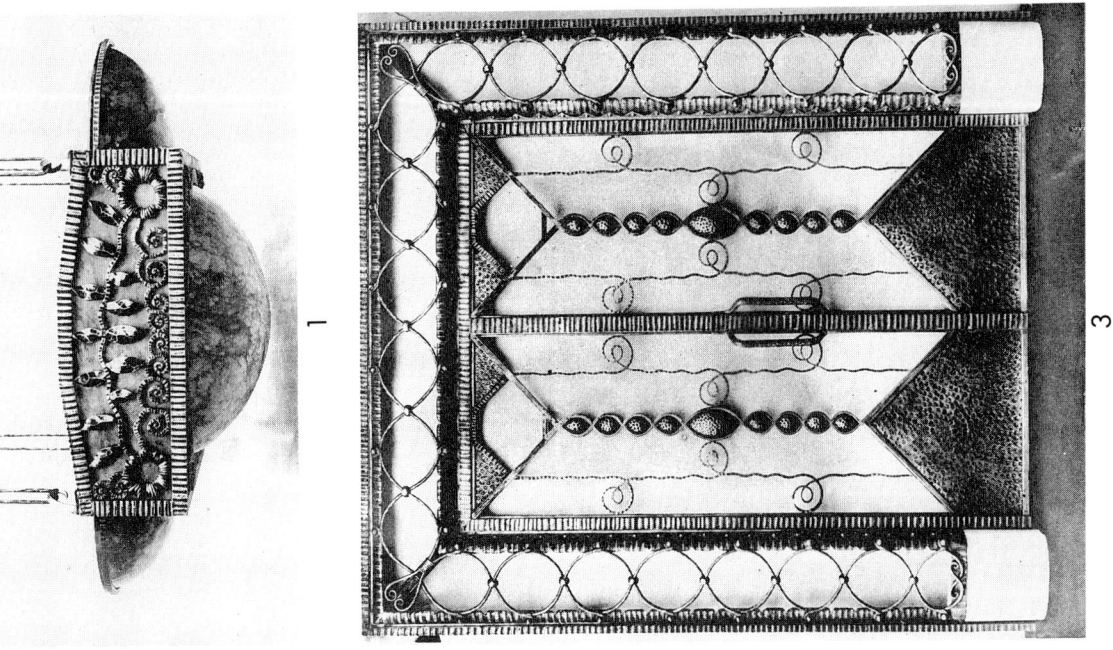

85.   Nics Frères. (1) Chandelier. (2, 4) Building entrances. (3) Entrance grillwork.

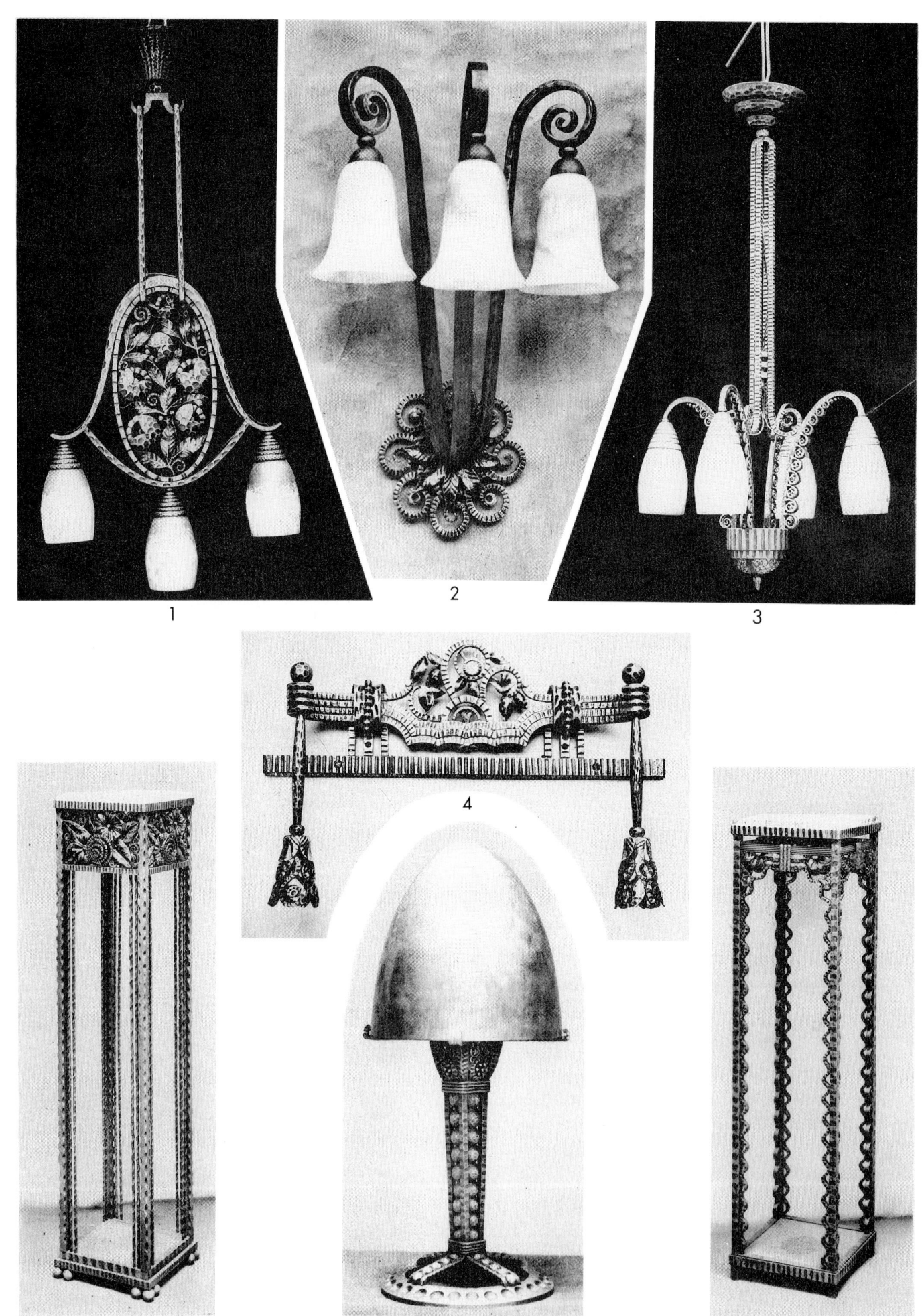

86.   NICS FRÈRES. (1, 3) Chandeliers. (2, 4) Wall sconces. (5, 7) Pedestals. (6) Table lamp.

1

2

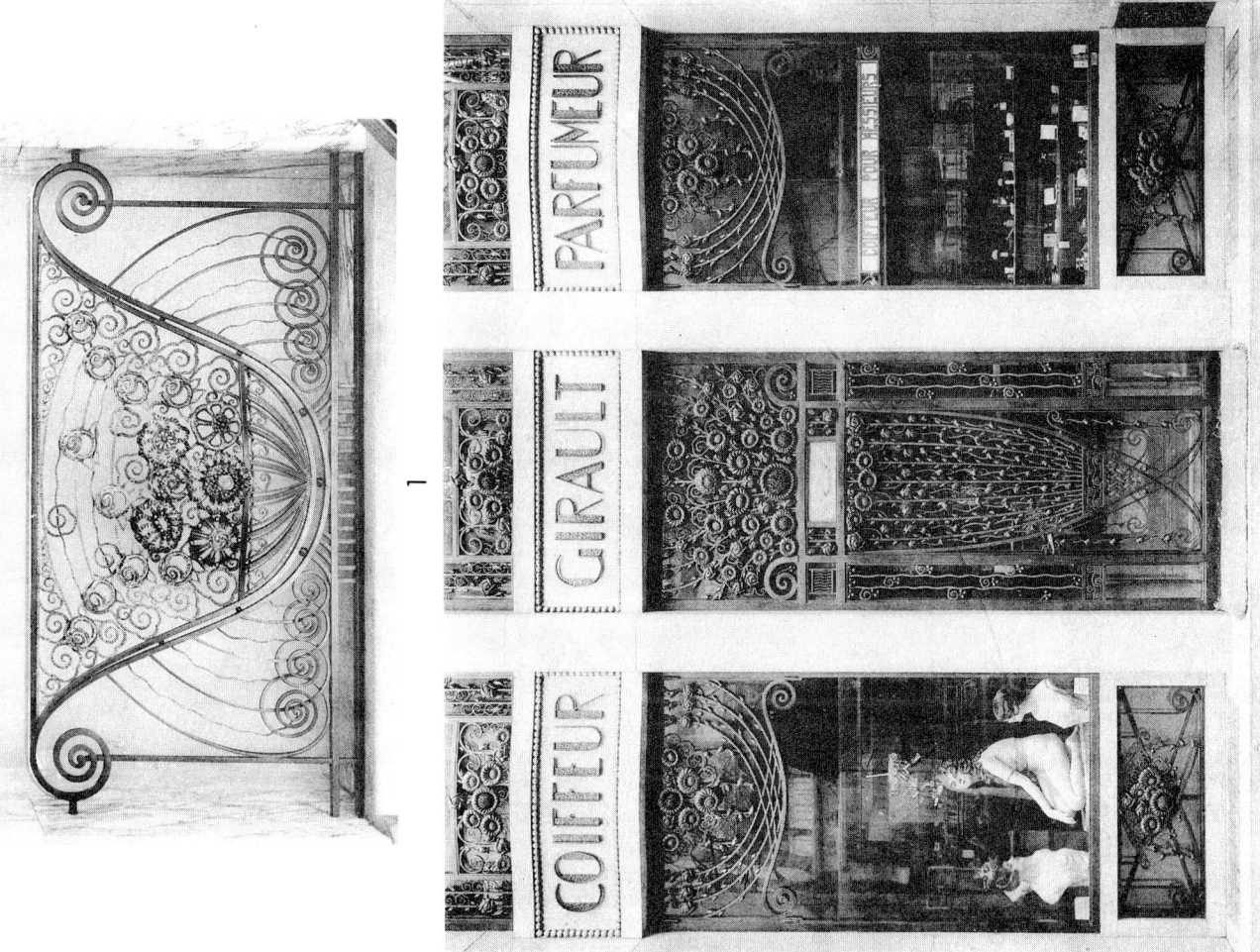

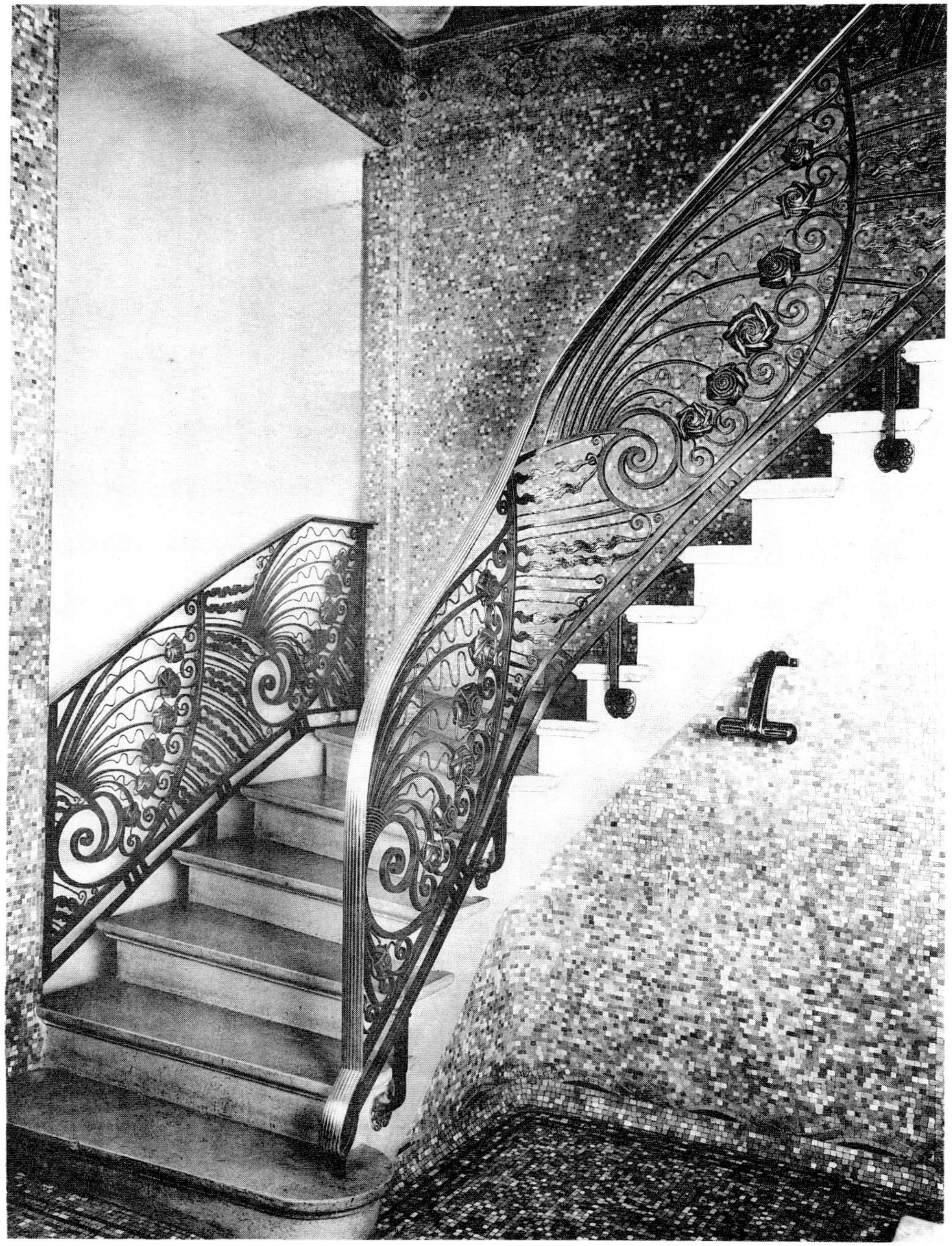

3

87. NICS FRÈRES. (1) Balcony. (2) Storefront. (3) Banister.

1

2

3

4

88.   NICS FRÈRES. (1, 4) Interior grillwork. (2) Radiator cover. (3) Fireplace screen.

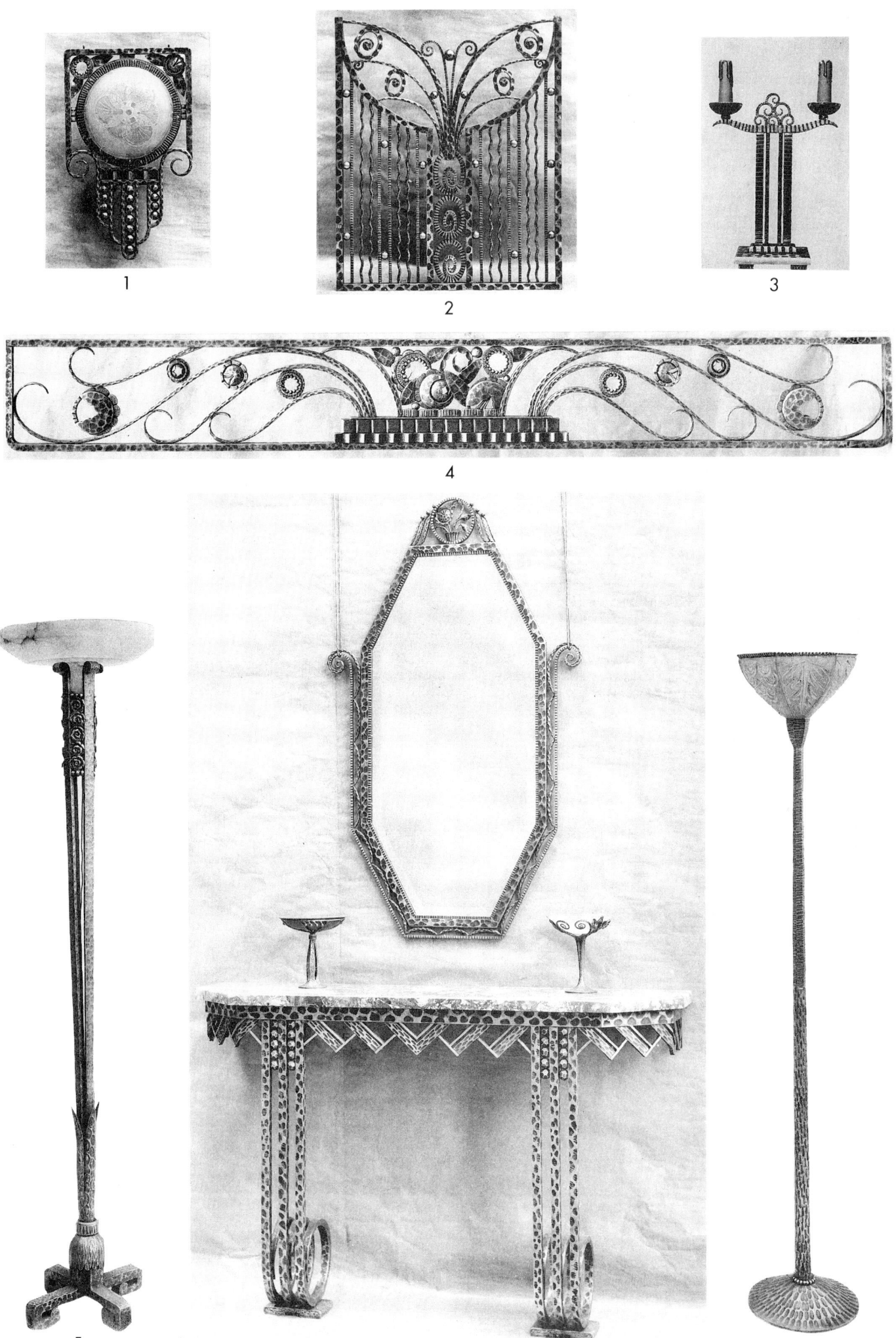

89.   NICS FRÈRES. (1) Wall sconce. (2) Interior grillwork. (3) Table lamp. (4) Fanlight. (5, 7) Torchères. (6) Console and mirror.

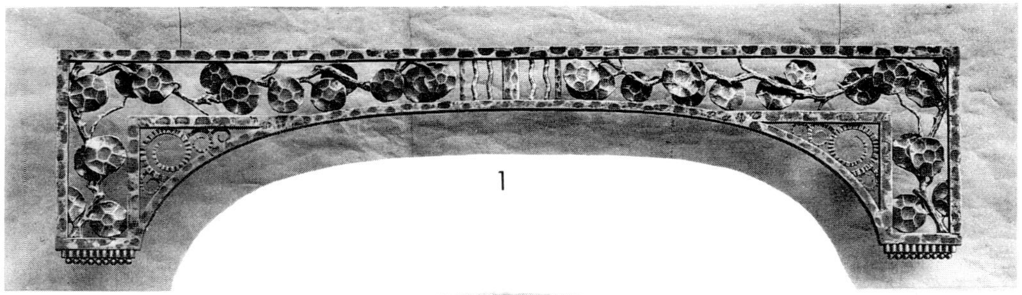

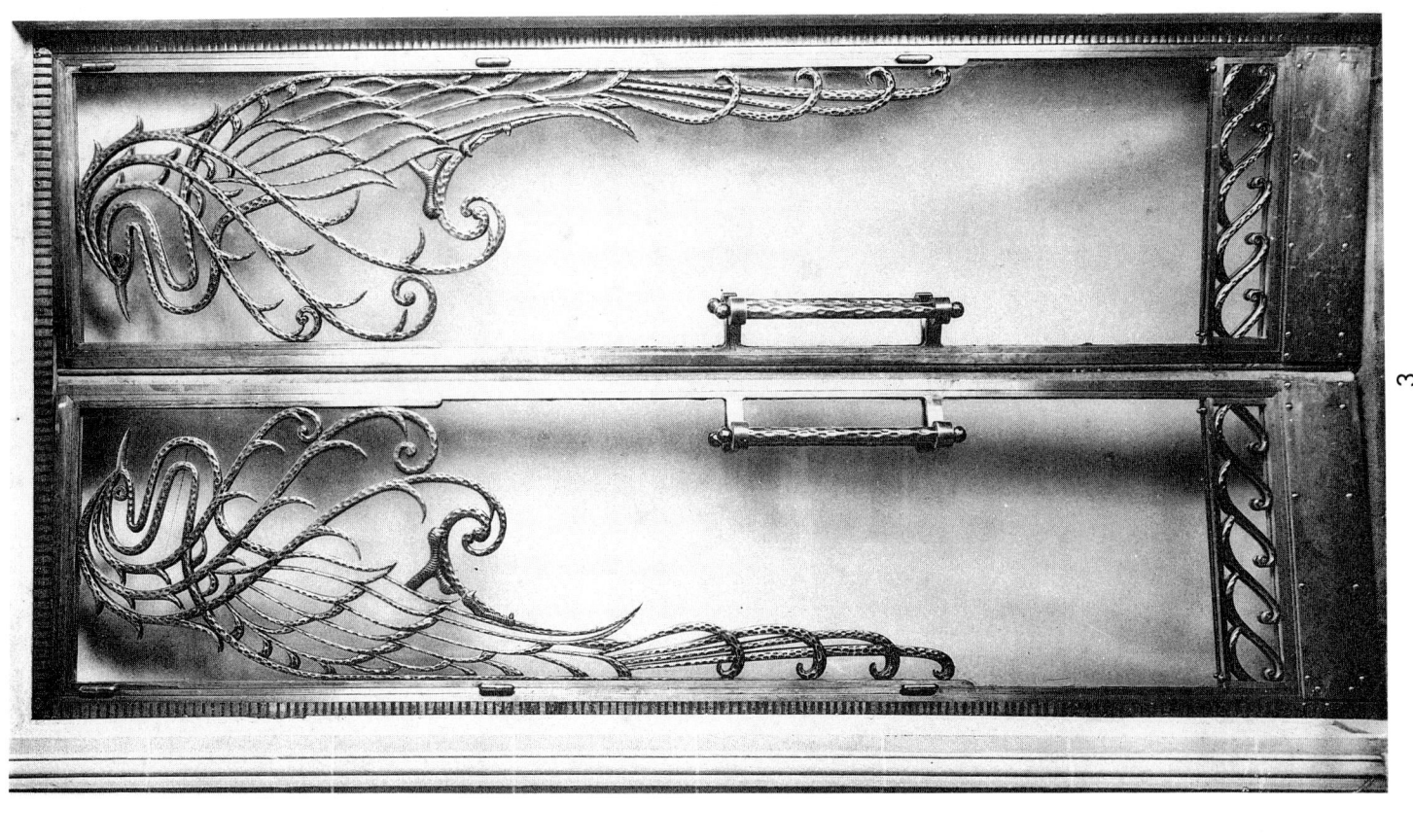

3

2

1

90.   Nics Frères. (1) Fanlight. (2) Interior grillwork. (3) Grille.

1

2

3

4

91.   NICS FRÈRES. (1) Console. (2) Side table. (3, 4) Banisters.

1

2

92.   A.-G. Szabo. (1) Chandelier. (2) Gate.

1

2

3

4

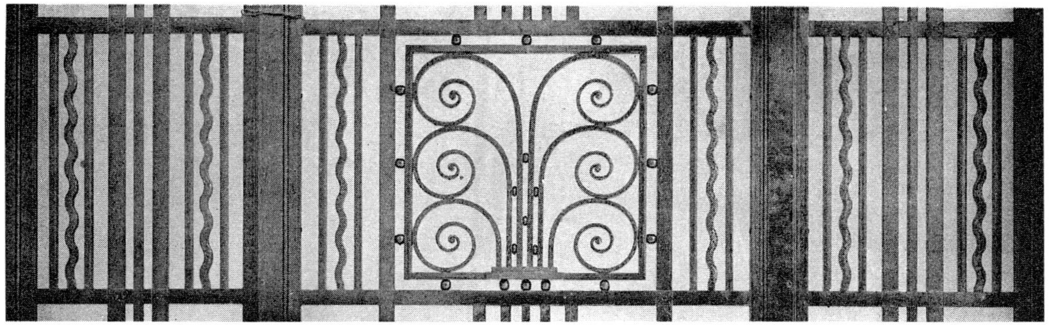

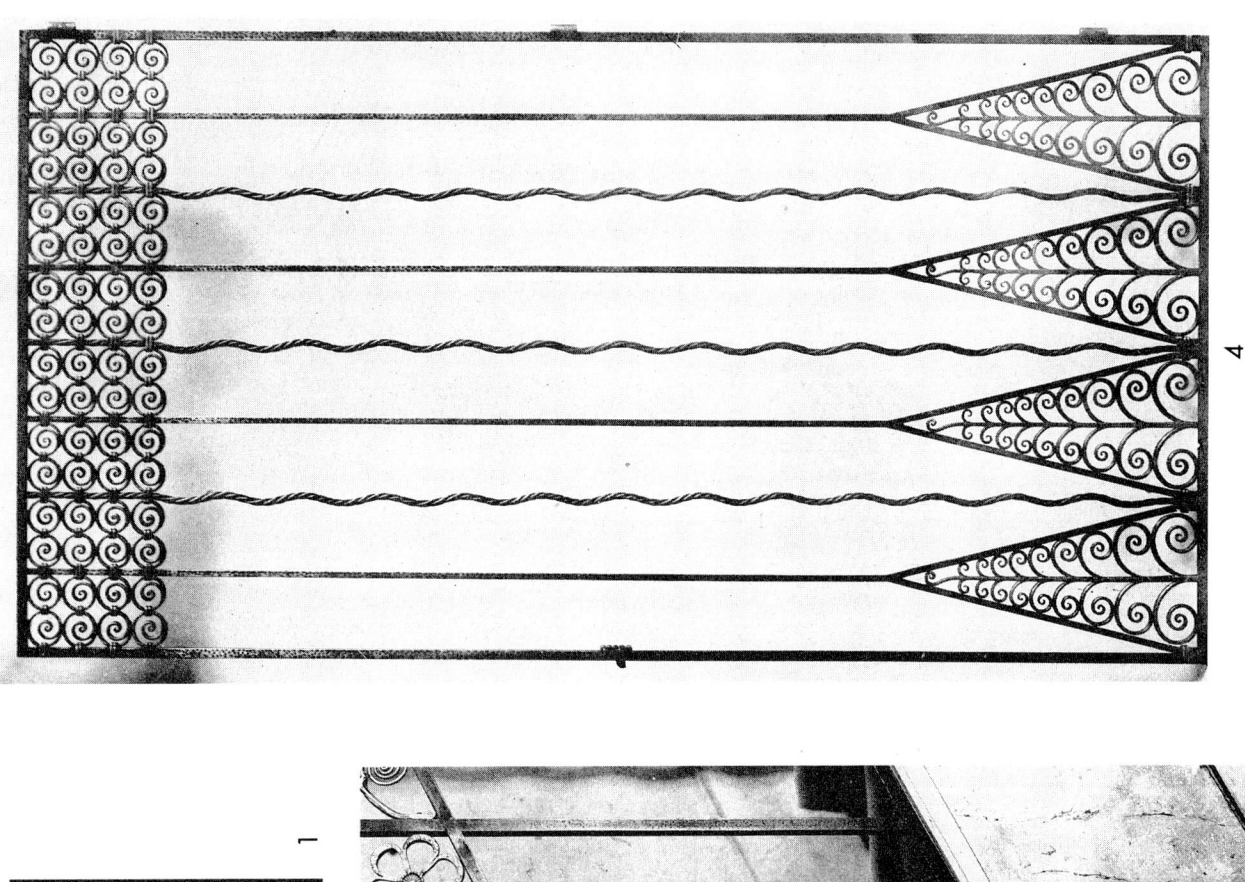

93. A.-G. SZABO. (1) Detail of a grille. (2, 3) Banisters. (4) Small grille.

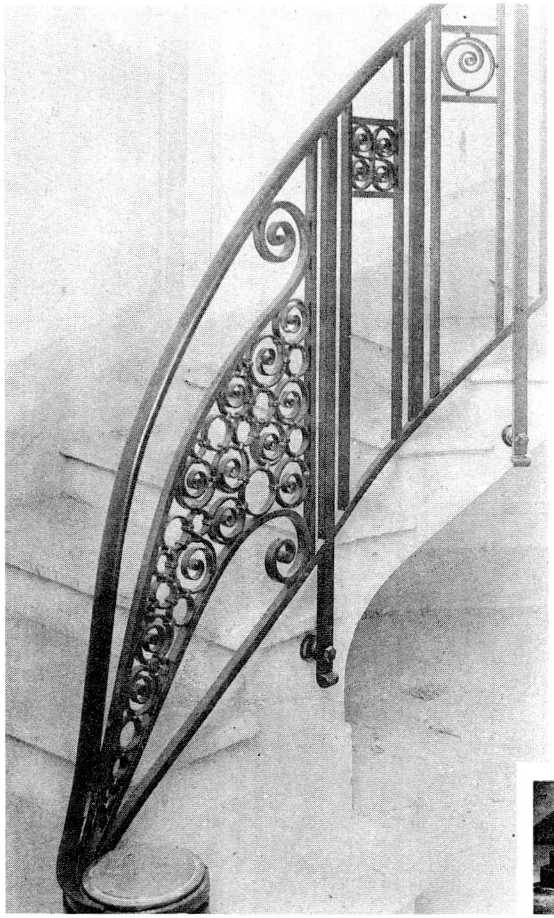

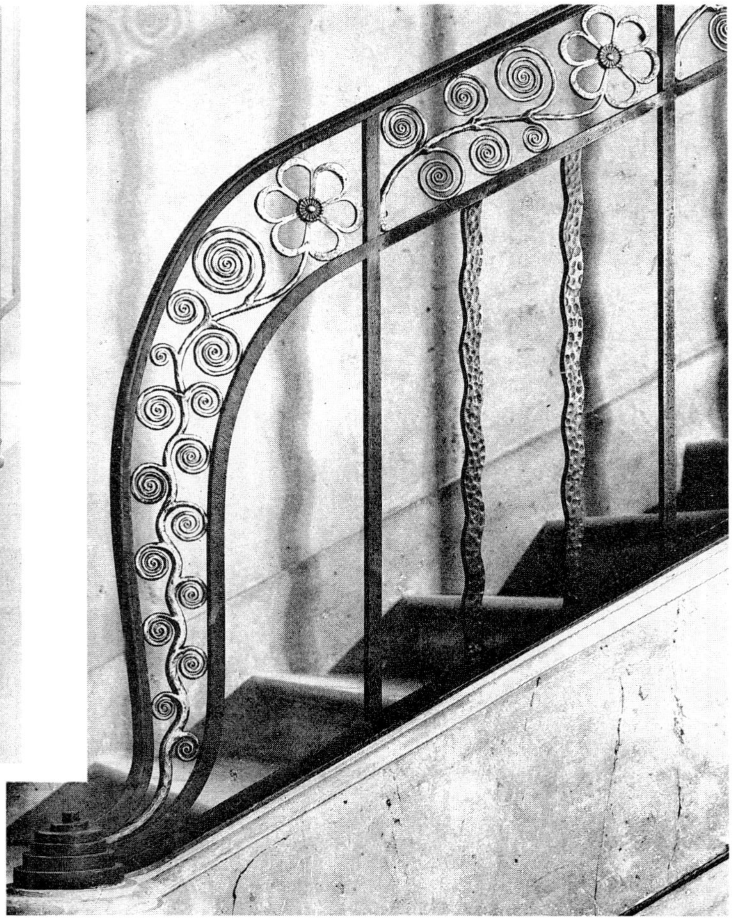

94.   JEAN PROUVÉ. (1) Interior door, Pavillon de Nancy. CH. DUMAS. (2) Entrance, Pavillon de l'Art appliqué aux métiers.

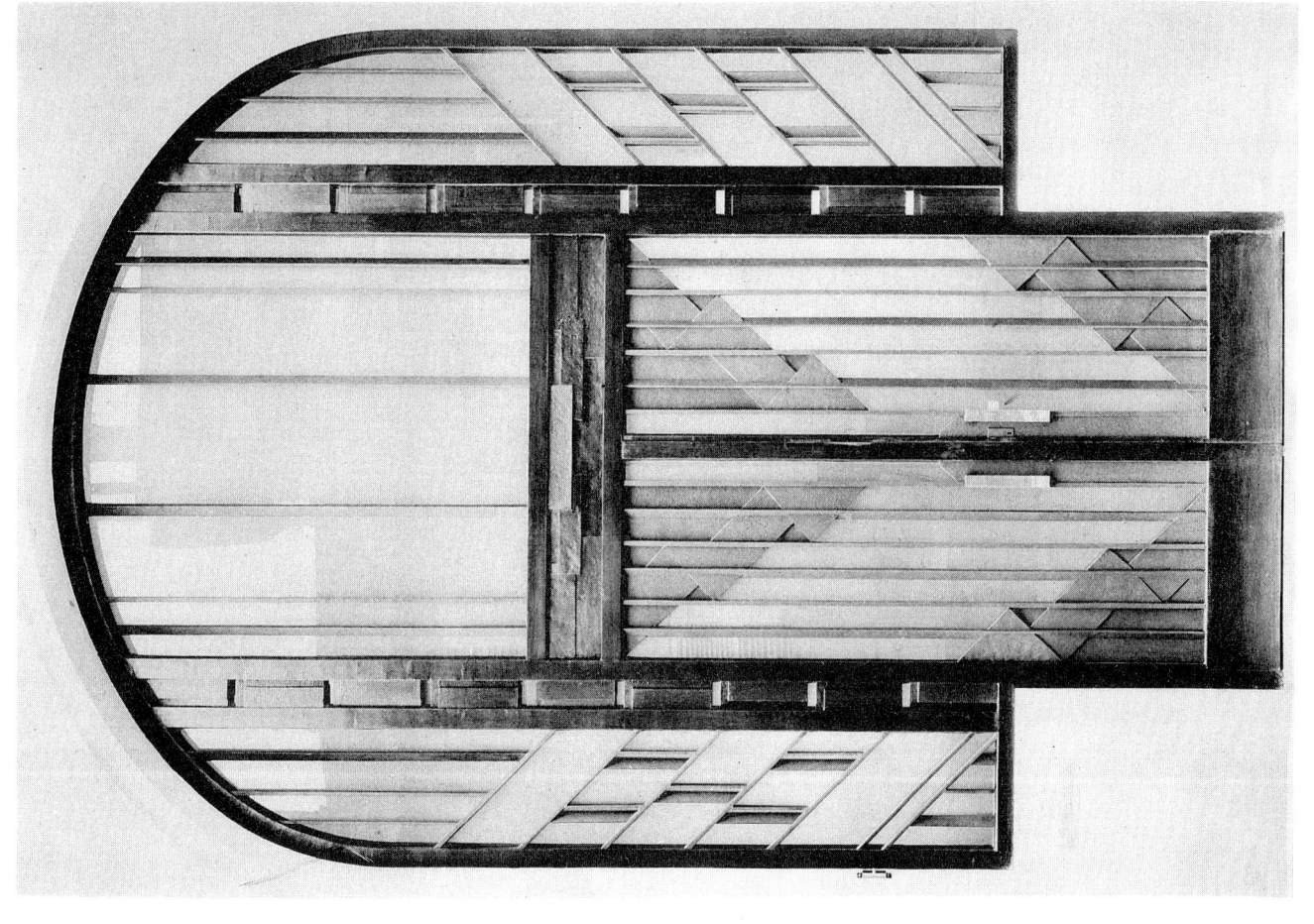

3

1

2

95.   JEAN PROUVÉ. (1, 2) Railings. (3) Door.

96.   RENÉ GOBERT. (1) Fanlight. (2) Elevator grillwork. ED. DELION. (3) Chandelier. (4) Interior door.

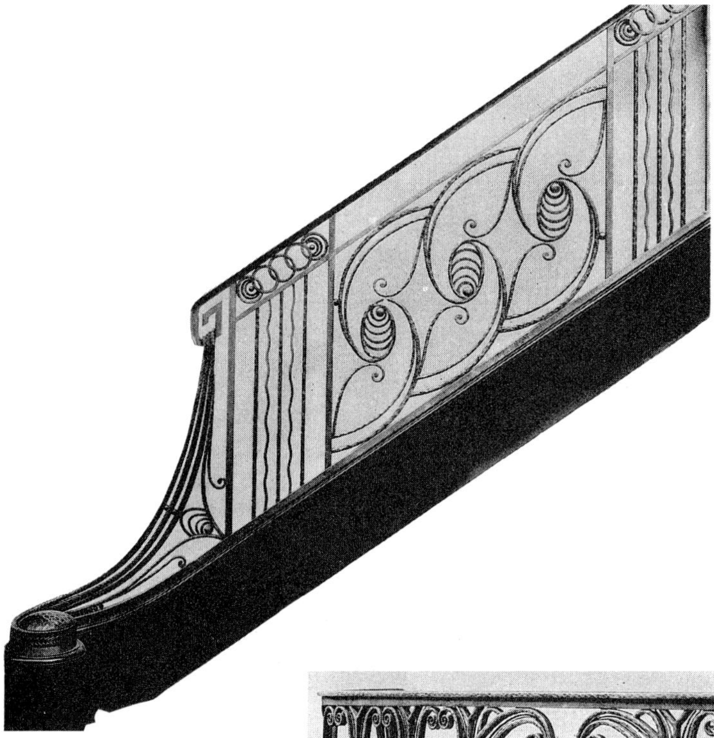

1

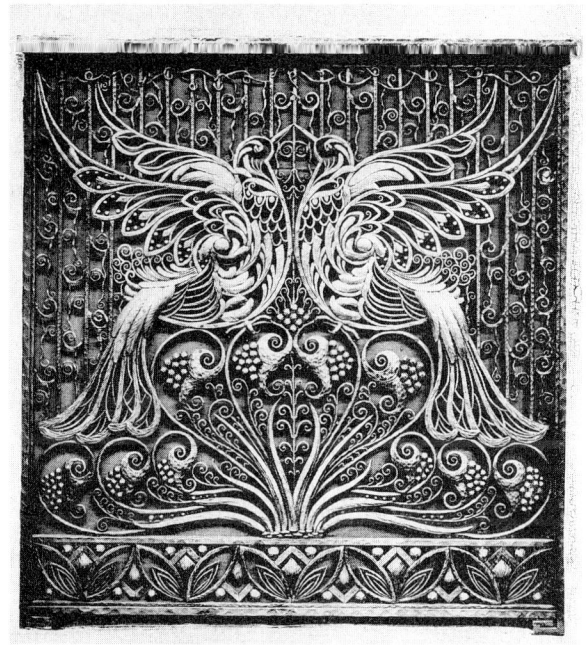

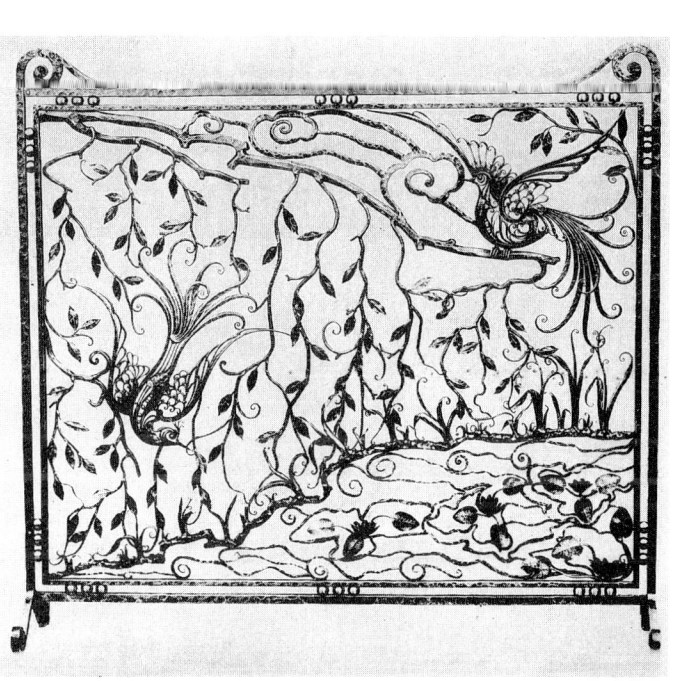

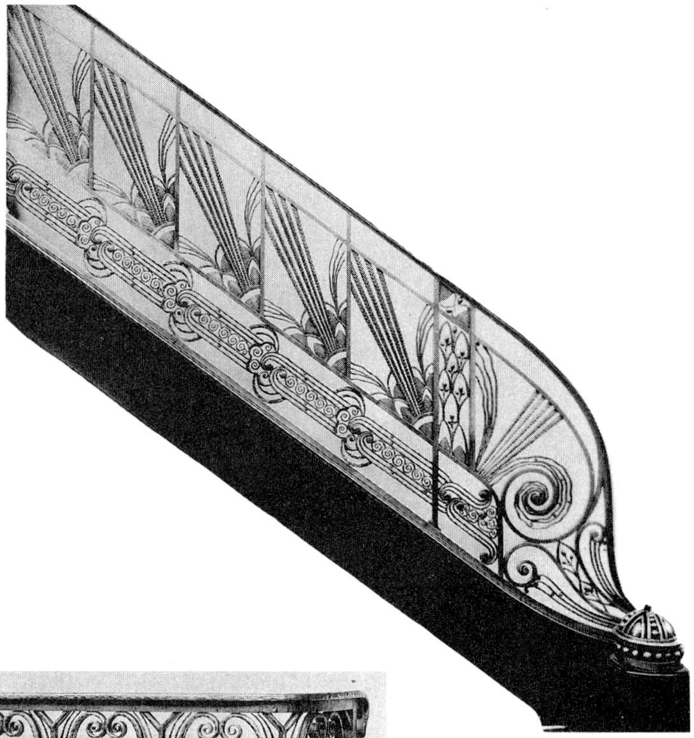

2

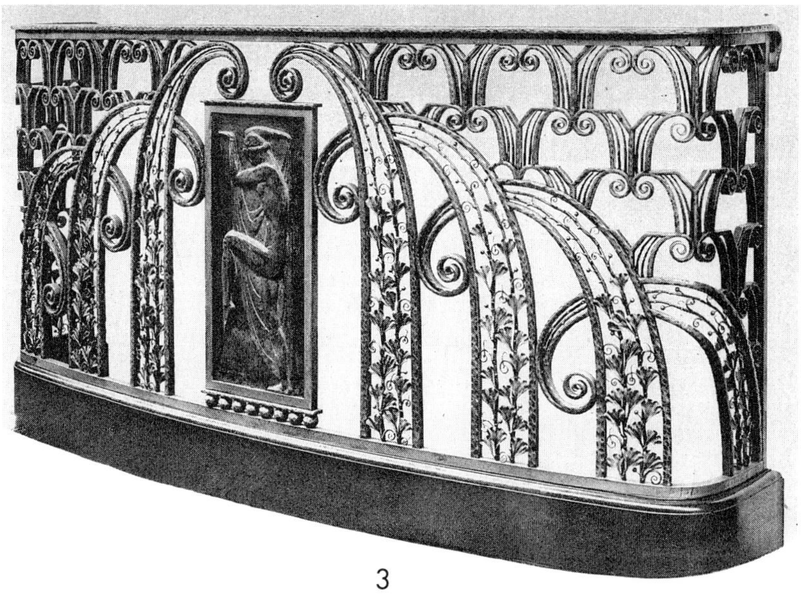

3

4

5

97. Ed. Delion. (1, 2) Banisters. (3) Balcony. (4) Radiator cover. (5) Fireplace screen.

1

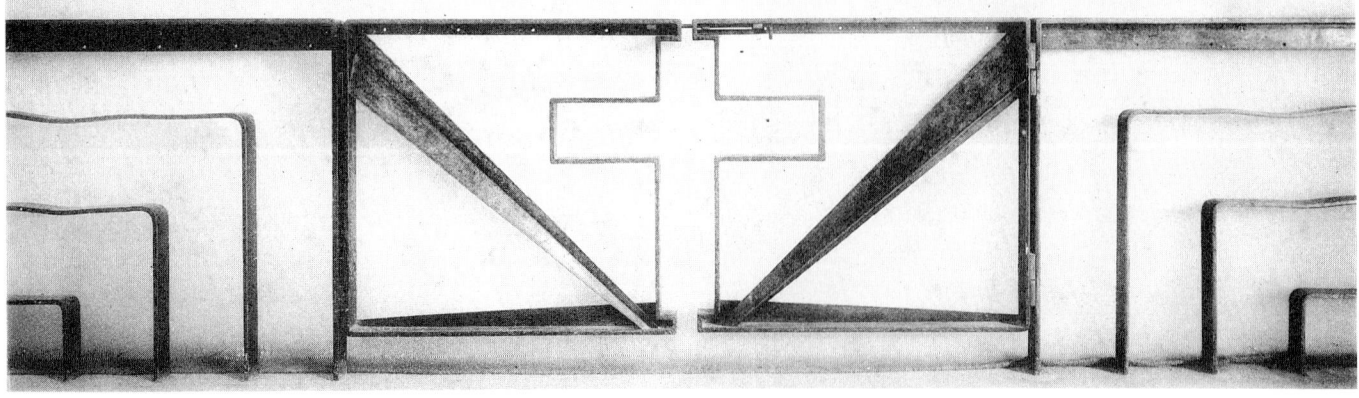

2

3

98.　Van Mullen. (1) Banister. Ateliers "Primavera." (2) Seven-paneled folding screen. Dalbet. (3) Communion grille.

99. Société des Hauts Fourneaux et Fonderies de Brousseval. (1–5) Radiators. (6) Radiator cover.

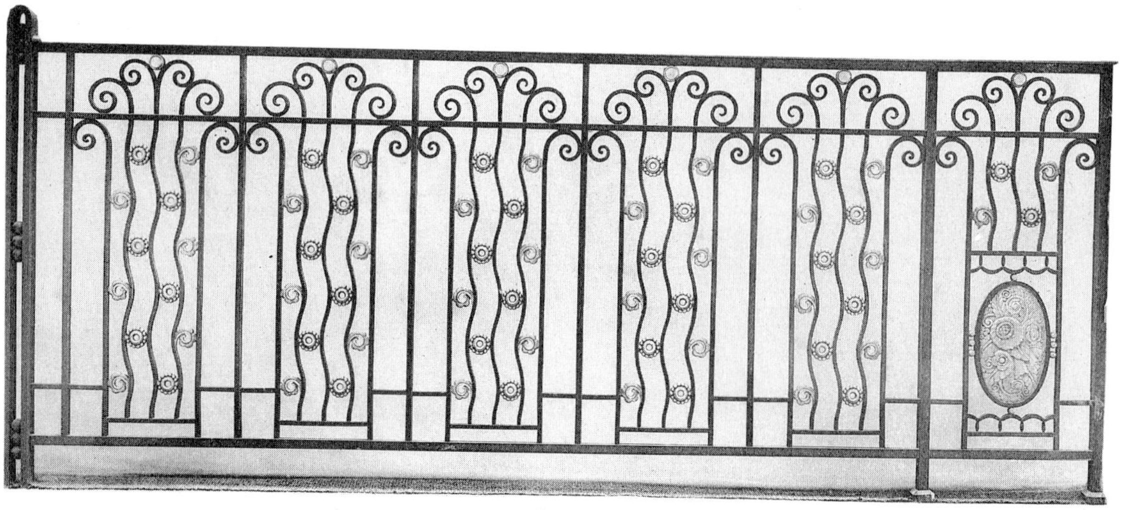

1

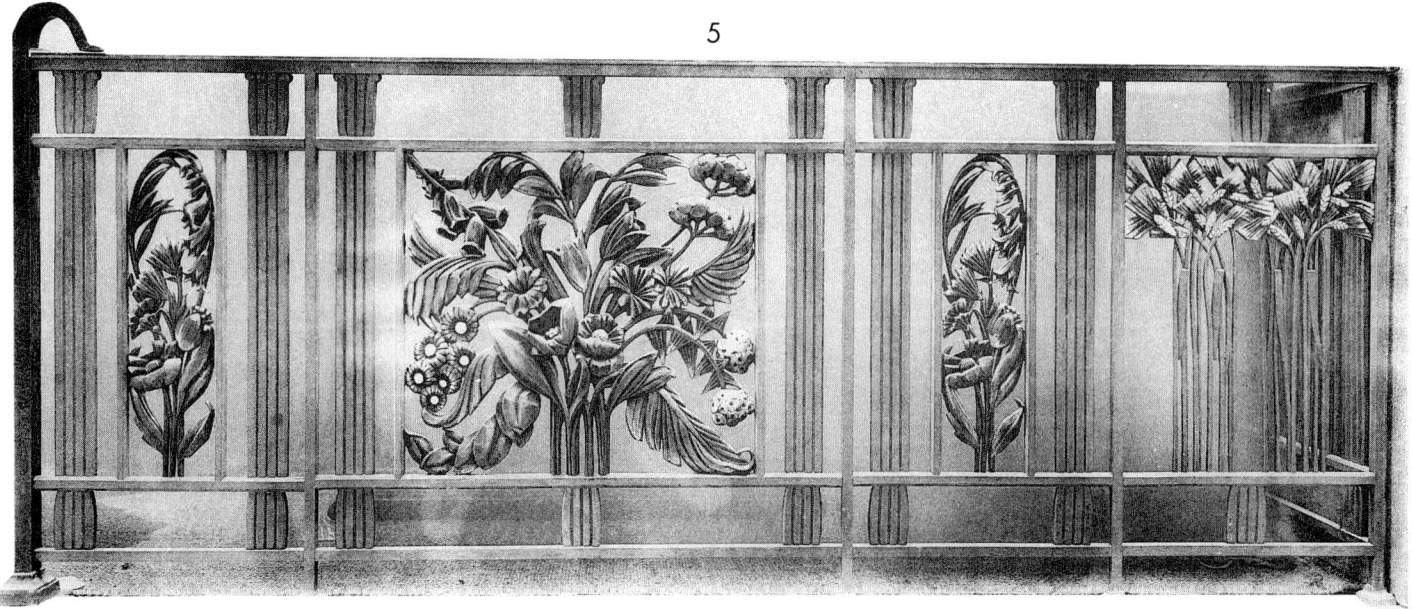

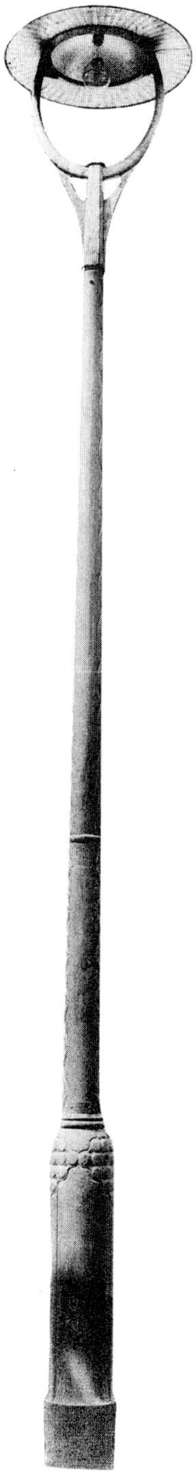

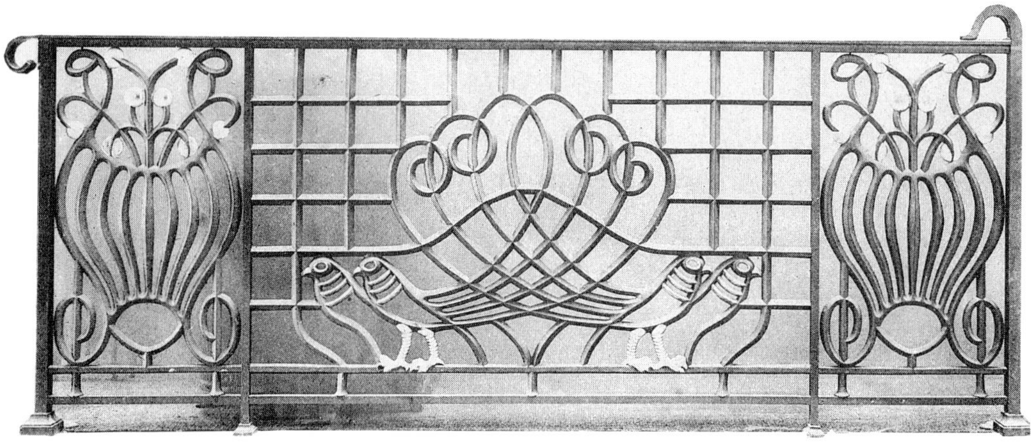

3

2

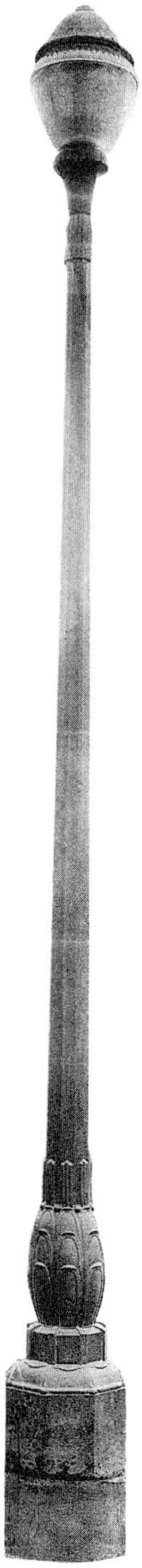

4

5

100. Fonderies du Val d'Osne. (1) Grille. Ets. Durenne. (2) Lamppost. (3) Balustrade. (5) Balcony. Ets. Saunier-Duval. (4) Lamppost.

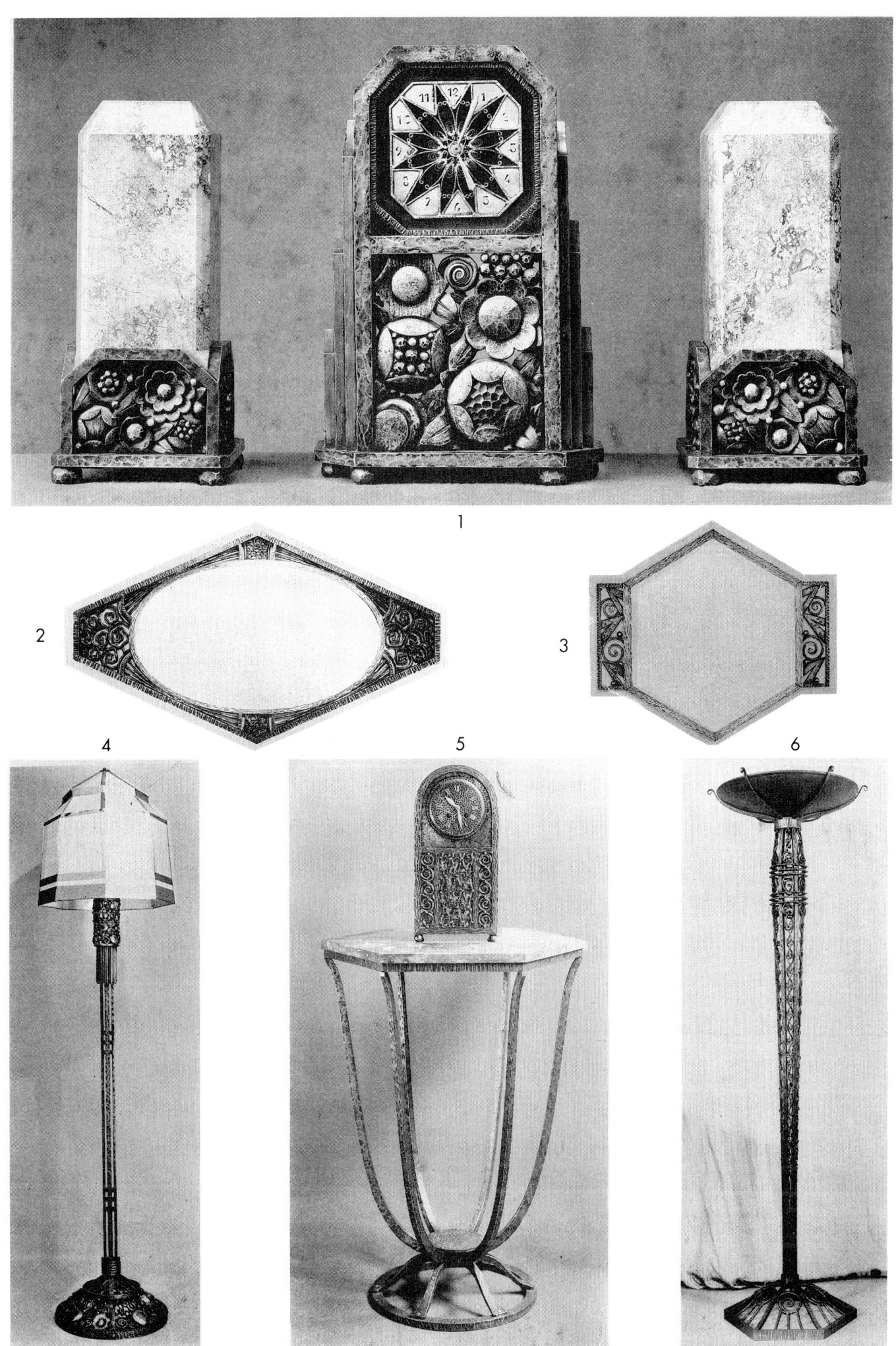

101. JEAN SPIRI. (1) Clock garniture. (2, 3) Mirrors. (4) Floor lamp. (5) Side table and mantel clock. (6) Torchère.

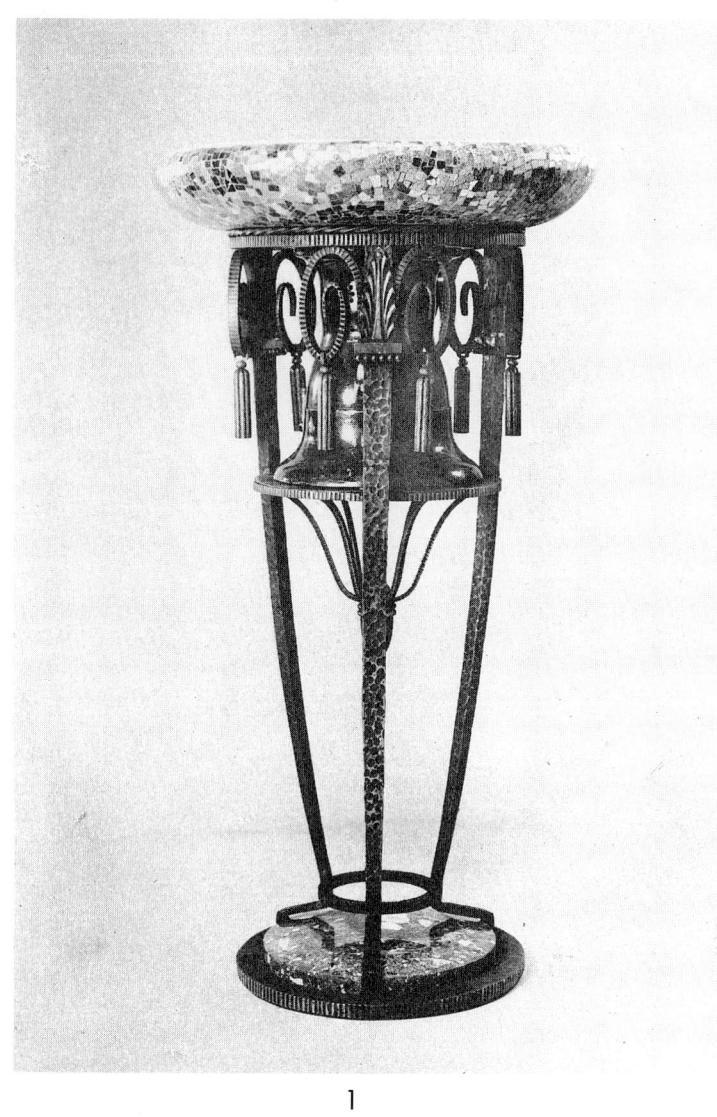

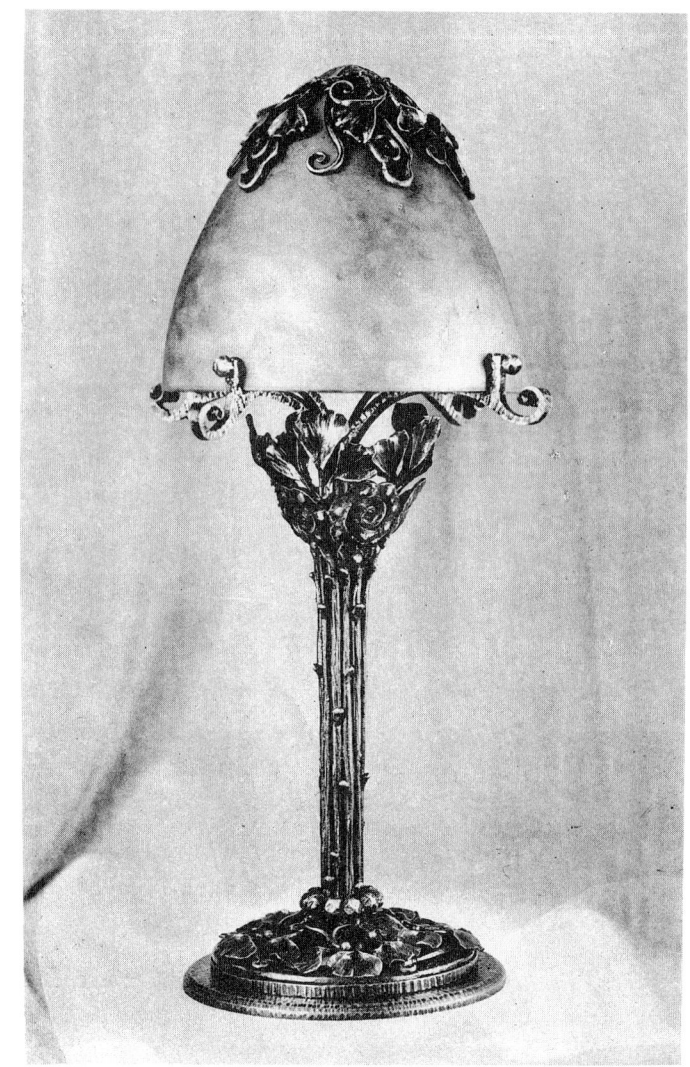

1

2

3

4

102.   PAUL LAFFILLÉE. (1) Urn. (2) Table lamp. (3, 4) Radiator covers.

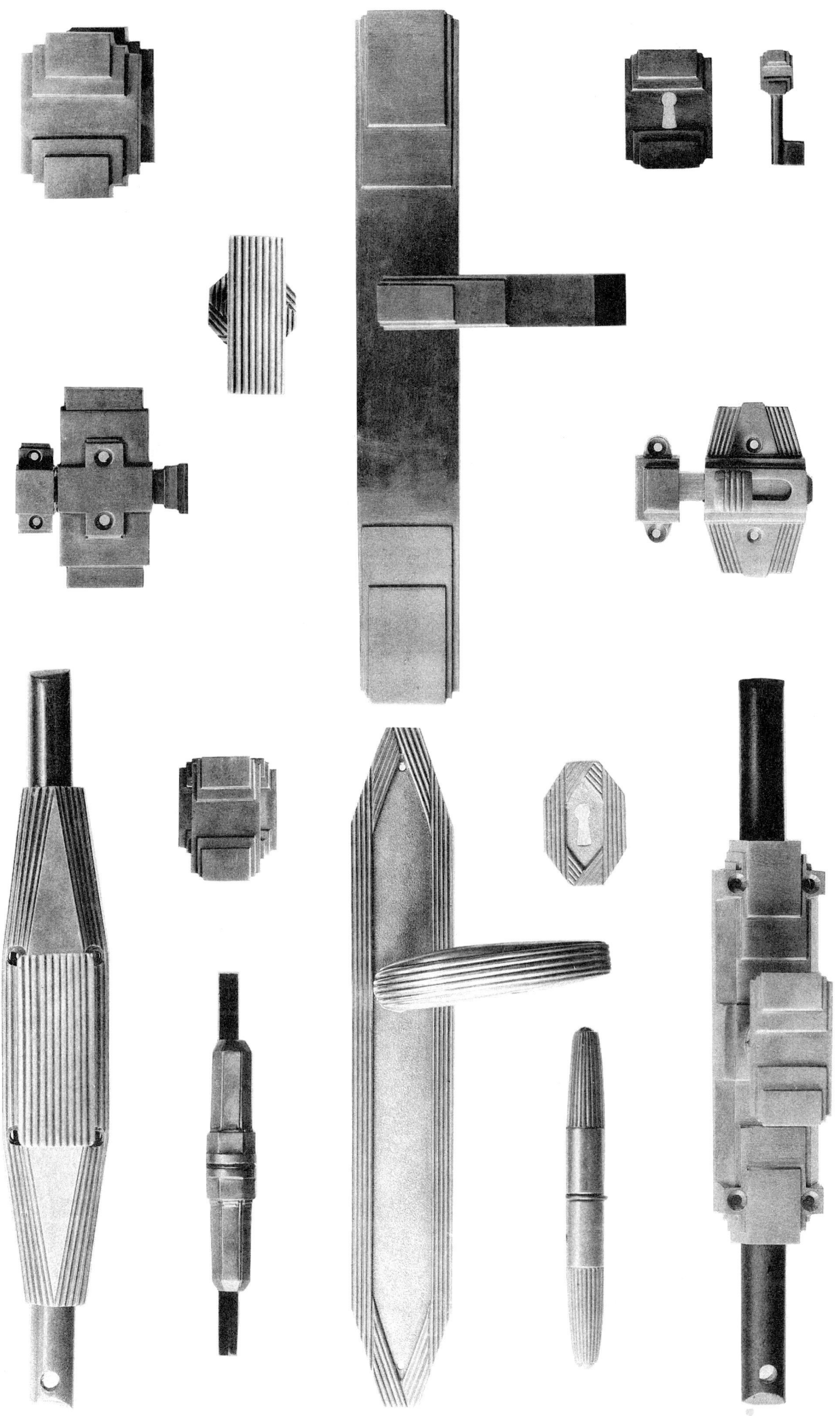

103.   Dominique and Jean Puiforçat. Locks and latches.

2

1

104.   PIERRE YUNG. (1) Store entrance. (2) Elevator grillwork.

INDEX OF ILLUSTRATIONS

(Editor's Note: The illustrations are classified according to subject matter alone. For a list of the featured designers, please refer to the Table of Contents at the front of this book.)